Repurposed Faith

"All of us can find ourselves feeling dry and weary sometimes when it comes to our faith and our relationship with God if we let the busyness of life get the best of us for too long. In her new book, *Repurposed Faith*, Rosie Williams offers a soul-quenching drink of refreshment for believers who need a reset for their focus and a reminder for their steps."

—Sara Horn

author of *My So-Called Life as a Proverbs 31 Wife*

"I highly recommend Rosie Williams' *Repurposed Faith*. This fresh devotional should be read with a cup of coffee in one hand and a highlighter in the other. To be candid, "quiet times" can become routine . . . even rote, if care is not taken in keeping this spiritual discipline alive and well. I especially appreciate Rosie's stories about her own father. Put this book by your nightstand, or wherever you read your devotionals, as soon as possible! The words in this book will spur you on to love and good deeds."

—Dr. Paul Pettit

President & Founder, Dynamic Dads

"In our noisy, race-paced culture, making time for the Lord is often the last priority. With wisdom and practicality, Rosie Williams shows us how to bring these quiet moments back into our day—and more importantly, why."

—Jocelyn Green
author of *Faith Deployed: Daily Encouragement for Military Wives*

"*Repurposed Faith* is a not-to-be-missed book that will cause you to rethink your approach to spending time alone with God. With honesty and vulnerability Rosie Williams challenges her readers to change the way they live out their faith by applying powerful Scripture, new techniques, and practical applications to everyday living. Don't miss this important book."

—Carol Kent
Author and Speaker, *When I Lay My Isaac Down* (NavPress)

"Do you struggle with your devotional life? Does your mind wander, your concentration lapse, your ADHD kick in? Then this is the book you're looking for. No guilt, just encouragement, personal experiences, and practical tips for faith-revitalizing quiet times!"

—Dr. James Congdon
Senior Pastor, Topeka Bible Church

Repurposed Faith

BREATHING NEW LIFE INTO YOUR QUIET TIME

Rosie Williams

AMBASSADOR INTERNATIONAL
GREENVILLE, SOUTH CAROLINA & BELFAST, NORTHERN IRELAND

www.ambassador-international.com

Repurposed Faith

Breathing New Life Into Your Quiet Time

© 2016 by Rosie Williams
All rights reserved

ISBN: 978-1-62020-558-7
eISBN: 978-1-62020-482-5

Cover Design and Page Layout by Hannah Nichols
eBook Conversion by Anna Riebe Raats

AMBASSADOR INTERNATIONAL
Emerald House
411 University Ridge, Suite B14
Greenville, SC 29601, USA
www.ambassador-international.com

AMBASSADOR BOOKS
The Mount
2 Woodstock Link
Belfast, BT6 8DD, Northern Ireland, UK
www.ambassadormedia.co.uk

The colophon is a trademark of Ambassador

Sometimes God places people in your life that are such a loving example of Christ, that their imprint is sealed on your heart for a lifetime. These people for me are Don and Glenda Mardock, my Youth for Christ leaders when I was an impressionable teen. It is to this couple that I dedicate this book with love. They mentored, taught, and lead by example a faith built on Jesus Christ and His solid Word. Their influence can be summed up as follows:

"Having so fond an affection for you, we were well-pleased to impart to you not only the gospel of God but also our own lives, because you had become very dear to us" (1 Thessalonians 2:8, NASB).

~ Rosie J. Williams

ACKNOWLEDGMENTS

I would like to offer a heartfelt thanks to:

- My Lord and Savior Jesus Christ for giving me the ideas, inspiration, and vision for this book.

- My parents in heaven, Andy and Erma Anderson, for leading me to the Lord as a young child and for taking me to Christian Booksellers Conventions where my dream to write a book was born.

- To my best buddy and husband, Steve, for the encouragement, support and brainstorming sessions.

- To my kids, Dan and Cyndi, John and Becky, Dave and "adopted" kids Scott and Lynn for believing in me and just for being you.

- To another "adopted" son Ryan Cavanaugh who designed my website and blog . . . as well as being the best tech guy ever!

- To my grandchildren, Andi, Wyatt, Benjamin, and Arthur for lighting up my life with overflowing joy.

- To my beloved friends Vicky, Pat, Kathy, Jayne, and Linda for praying me through on good and bad writing days.

- To Linda, Amy, Dorinda, Vicky, Lanelle, Steve, Jerry M., Jerry K., Polly, Pat, Tom, Margie, Bonnie, Barry, Kathy G., Sara, Rick, and John for sharing parts of their faith stories with my readers.

- To my editors, Becky and Brenda, for fine-tuning my words.

- To Tim Lowry at Ambassador International and his staff for making this book a reality.

- To Don and Glenda, owners of World Cup Coffee, for the comfortable chairs, Wi-Fi, and for not kicking me out!

CONTENTS

FOREWORD

We see it in others. An authentic connection and intimate walk with God. Their countenance glows, and it's obvious they have a growing faith. Regardless of their circumstances or personal challenges, they get it. You know they have tapped into their power source.

Perhaps at some point along your journey, you've experienced it yourself and know what it looks and feels like. The real deal. But for whatever reason, you sense a disconnect. The fire has died down, and the warmth of close friendship with God feels dull or boring.

Maybe you've never come to realize that the emptiness you feel can be filled only with the love of Jesus Christ Himself and that His love and grace is what you see in those people who freely live in it each day.

The bottom line is this: You want it. You know you need it.

The wonderful news is that He wants you! He wants to spend time with you and speak to you through His Word and prayer. It doesn't matter what has derailed you or what obstacles you are facing. What matters is what your response will be.

Through her own personal experiences, stories, and nuggets of Scripture, Rosie Williams offers inspiring and encouraging ways to refresh and renew your walk with God one day at a time. It doesn't look the same for everyone, nor will it necessarily look the same every day.

Whether in ministry to women, outreach to veterans, teaching Bible studies or serving at church, Rosie pours into people, sharing her personal spiritual journey and biblical truths.

You will be encouraged as you open your heart and experiment with some of the creative ways Rosie offers to repurpose your faith. My prayer is that you'll rediscover that meaningful love relationship you long for.

—Jayne Clark
Fellow sojourner & friend

INTRODUCTION

When something needs to be repurposed, it may be because it has lost its original purpose, become old, not valued, lost usefulness, is unwanted, is unrecognized, or is broken and has been tossed to the curb.

I'm reminded of a commercial where someone buys an old chair at an antique shop for a couple of bucks. The new owner paints it with bright paint, takes it back to the shop and sells it to the dealer for a hefty profit!

So what does repurposing have to do with faith? Just look at the list in the first paragraph of this introduction and see if you can relate to these descriptions on a personal level. Many Christians feel like they have lost their purpose when it comes to their faith. *Repurposed Faith* looks at a variety of causes for lack of intimacy with God and offers practical solutions from the Bible.

Lately, I've heard some of the following comments:

"I fully believed that God worked in the lives of others, and I could see it, but I didn't truly believe that God had a purpose and direction for me."

"I'm having problems, but it's probably my own fault. I haven't been in the Word for weeks."

"I need help getting into the Word. Although I know I should be having a quiet time, I don't know where to start."

"I feel like I am being a poor example to my kids or grandkids. If I can't have a meaningful time with God, how can I expect them to?"

"I know having more prayer and Bible study in my life is important, but why is it so hard?"

It is my prayer that *Repurposed Faith* will help people to remember the promises we have from God so that we can have renewed passion and zeal as we re-set our minds, hearts, and hope on not only the author but the finisher of our faith!

Note: Maybe you live in a country where you don't have access to a Bible or a computer with a Bible App. Pray that God would reveal Himself to you and show you that trusting Jesus Christ is the way to God. Pray that He would give you a Bible or lead you to believers who have memorized the Bible and can share verses with you. Maybe you can listen to the Bible on Christian radio or on a cassette tape. Remember this verse, "I will lift up my eyes to the mountains; From where shall my help come? My help comes from the Lord, Who made heaven and earth" (Psalm 121:1–2, NASB).

CHAPTER ONE

OFF THE GRID

Taking something ordinary that has been trashed or tossed aside and making something extraordinary is a popular and rewarding pastime these days. Just ask my husband, a self-proclaimed "garbologist" who has repurposed everything from an old sewing machine turned into a serving cart to a stack of barn wood given new life as a harvest table.

> *Repurpose*: to change something so that it can be used for a different purpose. From the Merriam-Webster dictionary

Or ask either of my two daughters-in-law who would not hesitate to dumpster dive if it meant getting something they could reclaim with a creative new vision.

It seems a lot of people have also lost their sense of purpose or value. Although they may have a genuine belief in Christ, they find themselves sitting on the sidelines, watching other Christians connecting with God in a vibrant personal relationship, yearning for a meaningful faith but unable to experience it themselves. Perhaps the disillusionment has come from watching Christians who proclaim an outward, Sunday kind of faith but seem to show no joy, love, or compassion in their everyday life. Perhaps a life change has left you feeling stuck in transition and confused about your purpose. Faith has grown weak and weary, in need of a face-lift and a revival. If we do nothing, chances are our faith will derail . . . something needs to change to keep our faith renewed and our purpose defined. Where can we find the kind of spiritual R&R we need?

The crazy noisy world we live in has people scrambling to fig-

ure out how to unplug from it all. Our circuits are maxed out with too much information, family demands, and distressing world events. There are so many distractions that we can't even think, much less slow down long enough to focus on developing our personal relationship with God. Quiet moments are rare, and we seem to have lost the art of simple listening. With our minds on overload, many of us are looking for ways to escape by going off the grid. Yet, when the quiet moments come, our overstimulated brains don't know how to react!

What would happen if we simplified life by unplugging from the chaos for a few minutes a day? What if we hit the refresh key in order to frame our day through a spiritual grid that would lead us directly into the presence of the Living God? How motivating to think about entering His rest or abiding in His love instead of trying harder to perform!

This book is not meant to lead any to go on the I'm-not-doing-well-at-having-my-quiet-time guilt trip that we've all been on many times before. Instead, it will examine what it is, why it's important, and why it can be difficult to have an effective quiet time. We will look at ways to align our life plan and purpose with God's in order to refocus our attention on the object of our faith—Jesus Christ. Studies have shown that the average church leader in Britain and the United States spends four minutes a day in quiet time (RT Kendall Ministries). People spend more time talking about the Bible than actually reading it for themselves. My desire is that when you think of quiet time, you see it as a springboard for meditation that leads to prayer and connection with God, a constant source of Living Water within that meets the deepest needs of your soul every minute of every day.

DO YOU HAVE A FRIENDSHIP (FELLOWSHIP) WITH GOD?

"I want to make one thing clear up front: having a quiet time does not secure favor with God. It is the privilege and joy of a redeemed heart—a heart that has already entered into friendship with Him through faith in Jesus Christ. If you have not yet repented of your sins and turned to trust in Christ for forgiveness and cleansing, I encourage you to do that now. Jesus has graciously invited each of us into his story; his friendship is life changing. This is the ultimate reason we draw aside to be with him. Not only do we draw aside in daily quiet time so that we might deepen our friendship with Christ, but also so that we might allow that friendship to impact us, to change our character into his." ~ Greg Herrick, The Quiet–Time: What, Why, and How (https://Bible.org/article/quiet-time-what-why-and-how)

Raised in church, I often felt inoculated with Bible verses to the point that I lost the wonder and amazement for the Scriptures. I used to make smug comments about the generic answers I had heard over and over in church sermons, Sunday school classes, and youth group meetings. Instead of the Bible being a living and active part of my everyday life, it seemed irrelevant, boring, and inactive. Having a quiet time of uninterrupted prayer and Scripture meditation was always something I felt I should do, but it was not always something I was doing or even wanted to do. Yet if you asked me to name one of the most important things I could do to maintain a close and personal relationship with God, I would then become the one with the generic answers: spending time with Him each day in meditation, prayer, and Bible study. I could point to verses like these:

But his delight is in the law of the Lord, and in His law he meditates day and night.

~ Psalm 1:2, NASB

The law of the Lord is perfect, restoring the soul; the testimony of the Lord is sure, making wise the simple; The precepts of the Lord are right, rejoicing the heart; The commandment of the Lord is pure, enlightening the eyes.

~ Psalm 19:7–8, NASB

In these verses above, the topics of restoration, wisdom, joy, and enlightenment were things I deeply desired. So why the disconnect between my head knowledge and my heart experience? It was apparent that when I stopped reading the Bible, meditating, and praying, I also stopped growing, but having this head knowledge didn't motivate me to apply this spiritual discipline to my life consistently.

I came to a place in my mid-forties where I was coming unraveled. I had a husband who needed me to be there for him. I had three sons, a demanding and stressful job, elderly parents to look after, a ministry to veterans and their families, a volunteer position at our women's ministry program at church, a role helping to lead an adult Sunday school class . . . need I go on? I tried to be in the Bible, but usually it was merely to prepare for a class or study and done in haste. My prayers were stress filled, pleading with God to fix this or heal that or help me just get through whatever that day held. I woke up one day, scrambling to keep my life from derailing, drained and overwhelmed with the sad realization that I had become lukewarm to the Living Word. I was not allowing the Spirit of the Living God to give me fresh insight each day so that I could receive His strength and guidance to direct my steps.

As the years went on, I began to see that there was a lot of the truth in those generic Bible verses from Sunday school. They were actually brimming with insight, and I marveled when God would show me a verse of Scripture that was so specific to what I was going through that I couldn't deny His care and concern for me. The Lord walked with me through those hard years and brought significant people and events into my life to teach and encourage me in my spiritual journey. I was keenly aware that the Bible was my lifeline to be able to hear from God, know how much He loved me, and discover how He wanted me to live. Yet often the quiet moments were few and far between. There was often background noise at my house, the coffee shop, or in the breakroom at work. I was still able to take a less-than-perfect environment, read the Word, and ask God to apply those Scriptures to my life. As I did, the meter of my heart began to go from lukewarm to hot.

A LIFE-CHANGING COMMITMENT

Although I became a Christian as a child, it wasn't until I was challenged to spend ten minutes each day in prayer that I began to have a consistent quiet time. I was attending a women's conference and the speaker was Becky Tirabassi, the author of *Let Prayer Change Your Life*. After sharing a powerful testimony of how Christ had changed her life, she shared her journey to learn about prayer and how to meditate on Scripture. She told us how she began to write down her prayers, inspired by reading the Psalms. She would personalize the verses and pray them back to God as she wrote them down. She gave us many ideas that we could use during our quiet time. I was drawn to her creative approach, as I had never thought about writing down my prayers. She challenged me to pray for ten minutes a day for the rest of my life. I felt the strong urging of the Holy Spirit to do this, but I am not the kind of person who can keep a commitment like that for five minutes, let alone for a lifetime. After asking the Lord for His help, I walked down the aisle of that Rocky Mountain church and made that promise to the Lord. I had no idea that the consistent quiet time I began that weekend would dramatically change my life.

The impact of that decision—to commit ten minutes a day for the rest of my life in quiet time and prayer—is why I'm writing this book today. There have been ups and downs since then; there always will be as I learn to walk consistently with Jesus. There have been days when I've wondered if my short bursts of prayers counted up to ten minutes. But there have been far more days when those ten minutes have turned to twenty, forty, or an hour, igniting my passion, speaking peace to my soul, and leaving me in wonder that I just met face-to-face—albeit dimly—with my Lord. A verse that I was immune to before became a kaleidoscope of truth and insight. The words on the page went from black and white to high definition color in my heart and soul as I received personal, life-changing words of love and affirmation from my Creator. Once my head knowledge became a heart experience, I was drawn even more to those quiet times.

PERSONALIZE YOUR TIME WITH GOD

Recently, when asking friends in our small group from church how things were going in their quiet times, one of the guys threw a question back at me. "That depends on how you define that. Because I used to have a structured quiet time and, honestly, I got bored with it. So now I have a different focus, and my quiet time is not so quiet. If it is too quiet, I can't even concentrate. I find these days my quiet time can be undisciplined; it's random. And sometimes, I have a great quiet time with my head on the pillow!"

This led to an interesting discussion that made it clear to me how different we all were in the pursuit of God, and that while I want to encourage believers to move from lukewarm to red-hot, there is not a neat formula for that . . . only Scriptures that are unique and personal based on the personality and gifts God has given to us.

One guy said that he had great times with the Lord when he was mowing the grass, as he was free of distractions and able to just commune with God. One of the women in our group shared that when she was a young busy mom, someone had suggested that when she was washing dishes, that might be a good time for her to pray and meditate. With each dish, she turned over, she prayed for something or someone. The chore she had once dreaded became a meaningful time for her spiritually and drew her closer to the Lord. One lady had a structured time set aside where she prayed certain prayers daily and used a more formalized system of meditation and prayer. One person mentioned that he felt he was always preparing for a class or Bible study, and that was not the same as just one-on-one communion with God. One person saw her quiet time as a more informal time, opening the Bible and asking God to direct as she highlighted, cross-referenced verses, and used that as a springboard into prayer. One man shared his struggle with dyslexia and how difficult it had been for him as a young man, feeling like he would never be able to understand and study the Bible like his spiritual mentors. His victory came as he plodded away, pushing past the difficulty of reading and applying some practical study skills that were tools he could use to overcome his learning problem.

The same God who created us put His Spirit within us. He knows our thoughts before we do! He speaks to us in unique and miraculous ways and is waiting at the door of our heart to commune with us if we simply come to Him with an open heart.

CHAPTER TWO

WHAT EXACTLY IS A QUIET TIME

WHY IS IT IMPORTANT AND WHY IS IT SO HARD?

WHAT IS A QUIET TIME?

In *Every Man a Warrior,* Lonnie Berger describes loving God as "the foundational cornerstone of your whole Christian life. To develop your love relationship with anyone, you must spend time with that person. The time has to be consistent and with a directed focus if the relationship is going to mature to a deeper level over time. It's called a quiet time, and there are skills that will determine its effectiveness."

Think with me for a moment about one close relationship in your life that was meaningful to you. How did you develop a relationship with that person? Are there ways in which building that relationship mirrors your relationship with God? I hope you have someone in your life who you love and trust enough to share your heart with, someone who is easy to talk to as well as listen to. I have found it is so much easier to stick with my quiet time when I remember that God wants to communicate with me on that kind of personal level.

Because we spent tender times together, I loved and trusted my father, and we were very close. For you, it may be someone outside of your family that you had or have a close relationship with or someone you respect and would like to know better. When we approach our quiet time as a conversation with someone we love, it ceases to be something we have to try harder to accomplish and instead becomes a natural interaction we look forward to.

When one of my family members or friends calls and wants to catch up over coffee, I don't hesitate to accept the invitation. The best part is being able to be myself, accepted and loved. Sadly, I have talked to people who don't feel so comfortable going to God. It is not a matter of trying harder to win His favor or grace . . . as believers, we already have that. It's *because* we have His grace that He wants to relate to us as a friend. The truth is that we have a friend (Jesus) that sticks closer than a brother (Prov. 18:24) who invites us to fellowship with Him any time, day or night. If we can grasp the importance of developing our love relationship with God as the motivating reason for meditating on His Word, we are well on our way to moving past lukewarm to a vibrant, personal, and meaningful relationship with God.

Instead of seeing quiet time as something to check off my Christian to-do list, I realize that it is the foundation or power source for the to-do list that stays with me throughout the day. For me, not only is it a time of worship and prayer and meditation, it's the compass that gives me direction and the power source for living. The world we live in is tough, and God wants to shower us with blessings and surround us with His loving-kindness and protection. Even when I am convicted of sin that needs to be confessed, it is with gentleness that He pardons, forgives, cleanses, and restores me. "But if we walk in the light as He Himself is in the light, we have fellowship with one another, and the blood of Jesus His Son cleanses us from all sin" (1 John 1:7, NASB).

WHY IS A QUIET TIME SO IMPORTANT?

I believe the answer to this question lies in understanding and experiencing the power of the Bible. When we open the Word of God, the Holy Spirit can teach us as we read and meditate and think about the spiritual food that is satisfying to our innermost being. We become confident in our identity in Christ; we become refreshed and renewed as we confess our sins and bask in the joy of undeserved favor and forgiveness from our Creator. Our purpose is established as He directs our steps and our hearts become His heart. The more time we spend with Him, the more our character becomes like His.

I was fortunate to be raised in a home where my Christian parents not only read their Bible daily but lived out their faith at home and in the community. I remember walking by my dad and mom's room, and knowing one or the other of them was in there reading their daily devotions. There was something sacred about that . . . something that made me feel really safe and secure. My parents owned the local Christian bookstore, and I will never forget watching my dad at the Bible counter, explaining to customers the various versions and features of each one. I can still smell the cowhide leather on some of those Bibles and recall my fascination as I watched my mom stamp the customer's name in gold on the front cover. As each impression was made to personalize those Bibles, so each verse within can impress Christ's message on our hearts.

On more than one occasion, I'm sure my dad was able to share one of the verses he had read during his personal time of devotions that would encourage a customer. Dad was modeling for me why it is important to spend quiet time with God. By spending time in the presence of the Lord, the love from his encounter with God overflowed to those around him.

Once, some Bibles were stolen from the store, and a newspaper reporter came to interview Dad. The picture in the local paper showed him standing behind the Bible counter with his hands up in the air, like "What? Stealing a Bible?" But still he was grinning from ear to ear, because I think Dad prayed that whoever stole those soft leather Bibles would someday open one up and read it and have their life changed and their heart softened because of it!

Another memory I have of the bookstore is of a picture where Jesus is standing at the door and knocking. "Look! I stand at the door and knock. If you hear my voice and open the door, I will come in, and we will share a meal together as friends" (Rev. 3:20, NLT). Today, I walked outside on my sunporch and found a bird frantically trying to find its way out. Poor little bird was panicked as it slammed against the screens. I propped open the door and tried to shoo it out, but the bird kept flying by the open door, again and again. Silly bird! But then I thought that's how it is with me sometimes. The door is open. Jesus is the door. Wow! Imagine that! It's not an unreachable "spiritual discipline" that He asks for, only that I open the door and let Him in.

HOW CAN OUR QUIET TIME MOVE FROM A GUILT-RIDDEN RELIGIOUS ACTIVITY TO A LIFE-GIVING TIME OF REFRESHMENT?

When I approach my time of devotions expectantly, asking God to give me something very specific that I can apply to my life, He never disappoints me. Some days He is silent, and I have trouble understanding the Scripture passage, but even on those days, I sense His presence. The Lord speaks to us through His Word, and we speak to Him through prayer. The Psalms are so beautifully written and a great place to start when approaching a quiet time. I love the way the writers share their human struggles. The gut-wrenching crying out to God is not some high and mighty spiritual utterance we can't relate to. Those cries touch very close to home, and we can feel the writer's despair. But just as real is the psalmists' faith that holds out hope and comfort and victory in the midst of life's battles.

WHAT PART DOES PRAYER PLAY IN QUIET TIME?

Donald Whitney offers some insight on prayer in *Praying Through the Scriptures*:

> Prayer is essential for the Christian, but it's not easy. Why is prayer so difficult? Why is prayer even sometimes boring? Why does five minutes of prayer feel like an eternity? Is it

because we are second-rate Christians? No! So why is it so hard to be consistent in prayer?

1: THE PROBLEM

Our problem in prayer is we say the same old things about the same old things.

We often pray about family and friends, finances, the future, work or school, church or ministry, or the most current crisis with ourselves or others.

Prayer is often boring. When prayer is boring, we don't feel like praying. And when we don't feel like praying, it's hard to concentrate or pray for very long.

These things are obviously important, and we can continue to pray about them, but in a fresh new way.

2: WHAT'S THE SOLUTION?

The solution is simple and straightforward. If God expects and calls His people to pray, then consistent, meaningful prayer must be doable.

PRAYING THROUGH THE SCRIPTURE

When we pray, pray through a passage of Scripture, especially a Psalm.

When we sit down to pray, we are responsible for creating the words of our prayers. When we use the Scriptures, the words are provided for us, and all we have to do is pray!

3: THE METHOD

Let the words of Scripture become the words of our prayers. For example, if we pray through Psalm 23, read, "The Lord is my shepherd," and thank Him for being your shepherd. Ask Him to shepherd your family that day, to guide, protect, and provide for them. Pray that He will make your family members His sheep, that they will look to Him as their shepherd. Ask Him to shepherd you through the decisions you must make about your future. When nothing else comes to mind, go to the next line, "I shall not want," and continue to pray.

Determine a set amount of time you plan to spend in your session of reading and prayer. Simply go through the passage, line by line, praying what you find in the text or what it brings to mind. If nothing comes to mind or you don't understand the verse, go to the next one. You may choose to spend a lot of time in a verse or move quickly through the passage. Nothing says you have to pray over every verse.

Keep doing this until you either (1) run out of time or (2) run out of Scripture.

Use the Psalm of the day. This divides the 150 psalms into five psalms for each thirty days in a month. Take the day of the month as your first psalm. Then keep adding thirty to that number until you get five psalms. So, on the 15th of the month, the psalms of the day would be Psalms 15, 45, 75, 105, and 135. On the 31st of the month, use Psalm 119. Take thirty seconds to scan these five psalms of the day, then choose one to pray through. If you get distracted, just come back to the next verse and continue.

~ Adapted from *Praying The Bible* by Donald Whitney
(www.BiblicalSpirituality.org)

My husband heard Donald Whitney share the method above at a men's retreat and started using this method about six years ago. It really helped him to focus during his quiet time and gave structure in his prayer time. Now he often will cross-reference a verse he sees in his study Bible, which leads him to other books of the Bible, and he will then pray a passage perhaps from the New Testament. It helps him to see the unity of the Scriptures and how the passages tie together.

WHAT ABOUT MEDITATION IN QUIET TIME?

As believers, it is important that the object of our meditation be Jesus Christ, not turning our thoughts inward, but upward.

I love the way David Ross describes Bible meditation:

> The one who reads and meditates on the Bible knows well that the Word of God is like a magnetic force. The Bible not only provides knowledge about God, it also draws the reader to itself for the purpose of meeting God.
>
> JB Phillips, when translating, was overwhelmed by the power of the Word of God, feeling like an electrician working on the wiring of a house with the electricity still turned on.

We meditate so that we can be caught up into the divine sphere of the radiance of God, and be so transformed by His Spirit that we begin to be molded into the image of Christ, the True Word of God. We then become "letters of Christ" to an unbelieving world, reflecting His image in our attitudes and relationships, and modeling His lifestyle, so that perhaps even one lost soul may see Christ within us and kneel down before Him in praise and worship.

A Table Set Before Me—*The Meditating Christian* by

David Ross

CHAPTER THREE

WHEN IT'S HARD TO FOCUS

I used to think that if I was a five-star Christian, I would get up at least an hour early and spend time with God in prayer and Bible study. Oh, I could do it in the evening if I was a "night owl," but that would probably earn me only four stars. Squeezing it in at other times during the day might rate between one  and three—and why even bother at that point? I didn't really think I could keep up with that early morning plan—or the evening plan, for that matter—so I found myself not doing quiet time much at all. Even though I tried a lot of different plans over the years, I was often distracted, easily bored, and lacked focus. My mind was overstimulated and racing, and it was extremely hard for me to pay attention. My quiet time was pretty much a disaster until I found a plan that gave me enough permission and space to be flexible and creative. When that happened, I found that as I was able to tap into the way that God created me and not compare myself to what worked for someone else, I could train my mind to be more focused.

I remember the day, many years after my kids were grown, that I looked at my health records. There it was, number one on the list: Attention Deficit Hyperactivity Disorder—ADHD. I don't know why I was so surprised. My family and I had joked for years that I had this condition, but my doctor never discussed it with me. I guess it was obvious to her, and she thought I knew it was part of my health diagnosis. Something about it being official seemed to help me put a name to my frustrating lack of concentration and focus, and my never being able to complete a task without extreme measures (as in consequences such as coming in under the wire on tax day)!

I will say that I have a high respect for those who rise early each morning for a concentrated and structured quiet time! I often ask my friends who are able to focus for ideas and tools they use to stay on track. I don't want to use my ADHD as an excuse not to put Christ first. And these days, I find myself sometimes getting prompted by the Lord to get up in the wee hours to seek incredible time with Him. I think this is so effective for me because of the freedom from the distractions of the day. I so admire the disciplined way that some people can meditate and study. At the same time, I believe that God has designed us differently, and we don't all have the ability to focus our attention in the same way.

For people with ADHD or who have trouble focusing, trying to have a quiet time can be a recipe for failure. I remember reading a book once about how to efficiently clean my house. The author said that the people reading the book who had ADHD would probably never finish it. I decided to prove her wrong, as I really was interested in the topic. The truth? I never did finish reading that book, and I have no idea what happened to it!

Just recently, I decided to stop and pick up some groceries at Walmart. My husband, ready to conquer this task with me, asked if I had my shopping list. After digging through my purse, I found a list and handed it to him. That's when the shopping trip started to go south. Part of the items on that paper I had already purchased earlier in the week. My random to-do list was also scribbled in. I then remembered that part of my list was on my nifty phone app for shopping, so I opened that up. *Then* I remembered the guests coming for dinner in two days, and I started planning the menu for that in my head. (Stop laughing; it's not funny!)

My husband was in an aisle that was two miles long full of choices, asking which cereal I needed. I was on full-blown overload and on the verge of punching him if he asked one more complicated question like, "what do you need next?" We made it through that day without a full-blown argument, but the experience led to an interesting discussion about how I needed help. I realized that I have trouble asking for help, seeing myself as a "functioning" ADHDer. He suggested I start each day with "my name is Rosie Williams, and I have ADHD," at which point I did punch him!

My friend Vicky is a master's level social worker and tells a story about how ADHD affected her at work one day. At one of the staff meetings, her supervisor had told the employees that they needed to organize their work space, especially clearing off the top of their desks. Vicky had recently been given the assignment of writing an article for the hospital newsletter. However, she took up the challenge and began to clean off her desk, determined not to do another thing until she was done. She realized that she left things on the top of her desk to remind her to finish a task, and she was overwhelmed at the number of unfinished items staring back at her.

Eventually, she got to the point where she was ready to work on the newsletter. After writing a few sentences, her creativity shut down. She sat there and sat there and sat there. *Nothing* came to mind. The harder she tried to focus, the more her brain shut down. Finally, she waved the white flag and went home. During the evening, she began to think of different ideas for the newsletter. The next day, she was able to go to work and quickly finish her article.

When I asked her what her takeaway was from that experience, she said:

- I had to learn to love myself and accept that God had created me uniquely. Until I could quit the negative self-talk about the way my mind worked, I lived in a state of defeat.

- The fact that I have ADHD does not mean I am not intelligent. It does mean that I have to reign in my brain with gentle reminders and helpful tools when it is firing on all cylinders.

- Instead of fighting ADHD or feeling guilty about it, I realized that it is not something you can change or conquer. I learned to see the underlying strengths and capitalize on that. The gift of creativity often bestowed upon the right-brainers of the world is not something you can control or schedule on a to-do list. Give yourself time and space to ponder, especially when it comes to spiritual things. God made you just like you are for a reason. Embrace that and please know that you are not alone!

THREE THINGS TO REMEMBER IF YOU
HAVE TROUBLE FOCUSING

- Don't give up! Winston Churchill, during WWII, was famous for saying, "never give up, never, never, never give up!" Remember that in order to develop our love relationship with Christ, we must nurture our time with Him. If we go to the extreme of giving up trying to have a quiet time, it can result in us drifting away from God, becoming lukewarm in our faith, and maybe even missing God's calling on our life.

- Before starting, pray that God will meet you in the Word or show you something new. Recognize that when we are weak, then He is strong, and we really can ask and receive help from the Lord to be successful. "I am able to do all things through Him who strengthens me" (Phil. 4:13, HCSB). "Now if any of you lacks wisdom, he should ask God, who gives to all generously and without criticizing, and it will be given to him" (James 1:5, HCSB).

- Make a commitment to spend at least ten minutes a day in the Word and in prayer. When I committed to doing this, and found some creative ideas to apply, my spiritual hunger was awakened, and I was hooked!

Even though it may be harder for people with ADHD to read the Bible, meditate, or pray, it usually still can be done. The Bible says to "set your minds on what is above, not on what is on the earth" (Col. 3:2 HCSB). The method of praying the Scripture mentioned in chapter two is especially helpful to those of us struggling to maintain focus.

Here are some ideas to help you in this journey. If you need even more help, consulting a counselor, a life coach, or doctor may be necessary.

SMALLER INCREMENTS OF TIME

I was told about a basketball coach whose team was a huge underdog about to face a much stronger team. Someone asked him what he told his players in the locker room before the game. He said, "I tell them just to play the next six minutes, then we'll talk. Anyone can play for just six minutes!" The coach would then give them instruction about the next short block of time and continue that throughout the game. Sometimes we also need a coach who can give us permission to break down a daunting task into a manageable time that we know we can succeed at so that we will not become discouraged. Try reading the Bible for six minutes, and then stop and have a talk with the Lord about what you just read.

If you are scrolling through social media, take a few minutes to open a Bible app and read the verse for the day. Ask the Lord to help you really focus on this one verse. If you get distracted, add a background picture to the verse and share it so that you can multiply the blessing of that verse with others.

My friend Tom is a teacher who has a lot of students with ADHD in his classroom. He says they are taught to teach by "chunking," that is, vary teaching methods and keep things moving. Lecture for ten minutes, show a video, have a group discussion, etc. If you find it helps, try chunking your quiet time until you find something that works for you.

If you are working, write down a verse of Scripture to meditate on during your break or grab that bulletin you wrote a verse on for further study. If you take a walk, pray the verse back to God and ask Him to show you how to apply this in your life.

Use a devotional guide as a way to get you started, but ask God to take you deeper, personalizing the message and giving you additional verses that relate to the same topic.

MAKE YOUR QUIET TIME A SENSORY EXPERIENCE

One of my friends listens to Scripture on audio CD and writes down any verse that catches her attention. When she stops the CD, she looks up the verse and records it so she will be able to remember where it is in the Bible.

I read where one person would write the location of a special verse on a smooth stone, and then put it in a jar. On busy days, she will grab a stone and then look up the verse. The tactical experience of touching provides variety and is a creative way to keep from getting bored or off track.

If you have artistic abilities, maybe you could design inspirational note cards that would encourage others.

If you are gifted with musical talent, maybe your time of meditation on the Word can be enhanced by singing or listening to worship music. I have a friend who puts on soft Christian music interspersed with Bible verses as she drifts off to sleep each night.

Maybe a verse or passage you have read can inspire you to write lyrics to a new song!

Eliminate distractions when you can, but if you can't, write down what you were working on and deal with the distractions one step at a time, adding some deep breathing and relaxing techniques so you can calm any anxiety you may be feeling. You may just find the distraction of plan B has a delightful sensory experience in and of itself!

ORGANIZATIONAL METHODS

Can we talk about organization for just a moment? I love big picture planning. I've used so many different organization tools over the years, it is ridiculous. My new favorite is the awesome I-Bloom planner—we will see if I can stick with that this year. But the truth is, I have trouble following through with things like that over the long haul. So my solution? If I get frustrated with something, I try to circle back and remember the tools I already have on hand and try once again to develop a habit of using it. My dad used to say, "The hurrier I go, the behinder I get!" I try to slow down and think through how to organize my crazy life. I am learning to say, "I need help," and when I do ask, my family and friends are more than willing to come to my rescue. But my most help comes from Psalms: "My help comes from the Lord, the Maker of heaven and earth" (Psalm 121:2 HCSB).

CHAPTER FOUR

PLEEEEEZE DON'T MAKE ME JOURNAL!

As I begin this chapter, I can almost hear some of you saying, "Please don't tell me to journal!" I know that would be my husband's

plea. We were sorting through the books on our shelf recently, and I picked up a beautiful black leather journal I had gotten him some years back. I opened it to see nothing but blank pages. Obviously, journaling doesn't appeal to everyone. Throughout this chapter I will share the affect that journaling has had on my life, but I'll also give alternative ideas. Keep in mind the goal is to remember what God is showing us through His Word. Some may do that through pages of handwritten thoughts, while others may jot down a few words on sticky notes as a reminder. If we can recognize and appreciate that there are many methods by which we capture and record our quiet time thoughts, we can find success in the methods we are most comfortable with.

A SIMPLE 3X5 CARD

In the past I've had numerous occasions to want to share with someone in need a special verse of Scripture, an application, or an insight that was meaningful to me, but I couldn't remember what it was or where it was found. When I began to be consistent about my quiet time, I began to write down meaningful verses with the date and my name on a 3x5 card, which I then filed alphabetically by a key word to help me remember it. Inevitably, I ran into someone who needed that same Scripture, so I would copy the verse and give it to them. This happened so often, that I began to write out two 3x5 cards: one to file away and one to tuck in my Bible or purse. I prayed that God would show me just the person who needed it. I remember giving one of those verses to one of my son's grade school teachers, along with a note thanking her for spending extra time with him in the classroom. I was completely surprised when I ran into her about twenty years later, and she pulled out that worn card from her Bible and said how much that had meant to her! I love how God multiplied the blessing of that one little verse, first to me and then to a special someone He prompted me to share it with. One of my close girlfriends also would write down verses to keep and give away. Little did we know how powerful those verses would be to minister to each other as we exchanged cards when various trials would come into our lives. On several occasions, God gave us the exact same verse on the same day. On several of those occasions, the verse was about God's warning to His people not to be "stiff-necked," and we had to laugh at God's sense of humor while at the same time saying, "What are you trying to tell us, God?"

LETTERS

One of the few people who ever writes me letters anymore is my aunt. It's sheer delight to find her familiar handwriting on an envelope buried within a stack of bills. It makes me stop, grab a cup of coffee, and catch up with what's going on in her life. She lives in a small, rural Kansas town and almost always relays something that's going on at her church that week. Her love comes through strong, and she always ends with an invitation to come visit. I used to just read her letters and go on, but eighteen months ago her sister (my mom) died. These days, I always write back. It saddens me that letter writing is almost a lost art. I have a special box of letters that my husband wrote home to me from Vietnam . . . not only did they express his love to me, but they also recorded his faith in God and the verses that sustained him.

Think about how many times Bible chapters begin with "As it is written" in Mark, or "Inasmuch as many have undertaken to compile an account of the things accomplished among us" in Luke, or "I have written these things to you who believe in the name of the Son of God, so that you may know that you have eternal life" (1 John 5:13, HCSB), or "Look at what large letters I use as I write to you in my own handwriting" (Gal. 6:11, HCSB), or my favorite Bible verses, "You yourselves are our letter, written on our hearts, recognized and read by everyone. It is clear that you are Christ's letter, produced by us, not written with ink, but with the Spirit of the Living God—not on stone tablets but on tablets that are hearts of flesh" (2 Cor. 3:2-3, HCSB). Letter writing is a way we can pass on to someone else words of love, hope and encouragement, and faith. Inspired by my aunt, I wrote a letter to my cousin the other day. She was so appreciative because the letter was delivered in the midst of a difficult and stressful week for her. As we take the personal time to allow the Spirit of God to write His words on our hearts, we can then be Christ's letter to those around us!

JOURNALING

When I first began to journal, I was challenged by Becky Tirabassi, author of *Let Prayer Change Your Life*, to make a commitment to spend at least ten minutes a day for the rest of my life praying and reading the Bible. At first I felt intimated as I looked at the blank pages before me. The Bible reading was something I was more familiar with, as was the habit of writing down prayer requests. The thing that was different was actually writing down my prayers and focusing on praising God for His awesome character. I primarily used Becky's *My Partner Prayer Notebook*. There are different sections that included a page of notes with guidelines for how to use it.

The first four sections of the notebook are my PART:

P for prayers of PRAISE

A for prayers of ADMISSION of sin

R for prayers of REQUEST

T for prayers of THANKS to God

The next five sections are for God's part to me:

L for LISTENING

M for MESSAGES

N for NEW TESTAMENT

O for OLD TESTAMENT

P for PROVERBS[1]

---

1   This excerpt is used by permission from Becky Tirabassi Change Your Life®, Inc. Excerpted from *My Partner Prayer Notebook* ©2016 edition and *Let Prayer Change Your Life Workbook*, © 2009 Edition, (p.68) Available at ChangeYourLifeDaily. com or Amazon.com

She also includes a to-do section so if my mind strays to other tasks, I can write that down and go back to the prayer or Bible reading without getting off track. Each section of the journal had a page of explanation, giving ideas for how to use it. Because the primary book to read when praising God is Psalms, I learned to pattern my prayers after the psalmist, and soon it became a natural part of my daily quiet time. I would write down Scriptures that were meaningful and then personalize and pray the Scripture back to God. The reading of the Word became a springboard for my prayers, and soon the awkwardness disappeared, and it became more of an intimate conversation with Jesus. I would get lost as I cross-referenced Scriptures, wrote down meaningful words and thoughts, and pondered the amazing way the Lord touched my heart specifically so that I would know it was His voice. "My sheep hear My voice, I know them, and they follow Me" (John 10:27, HCSB). When I gave the Lord just ten minutes, He often would multiply that time, captivating me by His presence. I certainly didn't have time to fill out every section each time, but the variations offered by each kept me engaged. The journal became a baseline for jump-starting my quiet time. I've used it consistently for over twenty years!

A SIMPLE JOURNAL ENTRY TEMPLATE

YESTERDAY

- What did I do yesterday?
- Did I learn any new application from the Bible, and if so, what?

TODAY

- What am I thankful for right now?

- What Scripture shall I focus on today? (Need help? There are thirty-one Proverbs, so try reading the one for the day of the month it is.)

TOMORROW

- What Scripture can I pray over my day tomorrow?

- How can I apply this to tomorrow's plans?

NOTES AND ILLUSTRATIONS IN YOUR BIBLE

I remember sitting in church and watching my dad underline Bible verses during the pastor's sermons. I was fascinated with the way he would draw squiggly lines to highlight verses and write notes in the margins of his Bible. I guess he was doing a form of journaling in his Bible before Pinterest made it cool! I also have enjoyed the Precepts Bible classes that use various symbols and colors to enhance the study of the Bible.

A fresh method I have used recently is Bible journaling. I have enjoyed being able to express worship and devotions in my wide-margined journaling Bible. There is space to make notes, create artwork inspired by verses, paint, or arrange die-cut illustrations sparked by a key word. Although I am not an artist, the scrapbook stickers from years past have provided me with a way to illustrate meaningful verses. I believe that God, as our Creator, has put creativity within us as a way of expressing back our love for Him, whether it be artwork, music, or even the structured, orderly notes of the left-brained thinker.

ART

My cousin Margie has trouble with Bible study classes that require a lot of detailed homework and study. She doesn't let that stop her from attending Bible class, but you may find her after class at her easel painting a watercolor that expresses what she got out of a lesson. If God has gifted you as an artist, consider how to give that gift back to God during your quiet times with Him.

MUSIC

The atmosphere of quiet time can also be enhanced by playing worship songs or hymns in the background. Because music often ministers to our heart and soul, it can set the stage for coming into the presence of the Lord with an attitude of praise.

AUDIO BIBLE

I have a couple of friends who like to listen to an audio version of the Bible. They will write down the verses that touch their heart and, after listening, follow-up by meditating on that verse, looking at the context for better understanding, or cross-referencing. People with visual impairments or who are simply auditory learners can benefit from this as well. I know a friend who goes to sleep listening to Scripture being read with soft music as a background.

NOTEBOOKS

Remember the guy who hated to write and had blank pages in his journal? That same guy, my husband, has been a Sunday school teacher for years as well as a small group ministry leader and state coordinator for a military ministry. He had to come up with a way to capture and record notes from his study so that he could use them later. He likes to cut and paste things from magazine articles, write down where verses are found under a topic, or do an outline of a class and put it in a three-ring binder. The more pictures he has, the better he likes it, so many of his notebooks are filled with photos that are reminders to him. When he is writing notes, it is like writing with his left hand, almost like dead time for my action-oriented guy. He finds it fascinating, though, that when he goes back to look at his notebooks, there are things he can use in his current ministry that he wrote years ago. That motivates him to continue as he sees the practical benefit. As he gets older, he also recognizes that the records he has kept will be a way to continue to share his faith to his kids, grandkids, and beyond so that they be inspired too. It is like trailblazing for this old point man as he walks in the Lord's steps and guides the way for those who follow behind.

THE DIARY

Realizing that the priceless heritage of our faith may be lost to our children, grandchildren, or great-grandchildren within a few generations makes me appreciate some of the writings passed down in my own family. My dad passed away thirty-three years ago, and one of my most treasured possessions is his little black diary. It was here that I read with tears streaming down my face how my dad had taken my mom to his pastor, who led her to the Lord shortly after they first got acquainted. I was mesmerized as I was propelled back into the 1920s and read about the faith they both shared, the verses he had scribbled in the margins, and the events that shaped his life and ministry. The most valuable reason to find a method to capture and record your faith journey is to pass it on to those coming behind you!

TECHNOLOGY

A few years before I retired, my boss began to train the staff on how to go paperless. That was a hard jump for me. I actually like to physically write things down, so I wasn't very enthusiastic about making that change. Now, as I observe my kids' generation, I see how efficiently they capture information and put it in an electronic file to be easily accessed with a few clicks of the keyboard. I remember a writer's conference I attended about five years ago where the break-out session I attended was on technology and social media. I was so overwhelmed, I had to leave the session early, convinced I would never be able to engage in this way. Yet, here I am a few years later using many of those tools that had so intimidated me. Although I love the feel of my Bible in my hands most days, it is nice to know that if I'm in a rush, I can pick up my phone and have a quiet time at the coffee shop or in my car.

There are numerous Bible apps available where you can switch between versions, look up commentaries, or share verses with friends. Instead of writing down things in a journal, a person could use voice recognition software to dictate impressions, Bible notes, or prayers.

Video logging, a private video diary, has taken off the last couple of years. Those that use it say it is a fun and reflective way to record and, if shared, can be an inspiration to others. This especially appeals to audio learners and would be a unique way to pass on your heritage of faith to the next generation.

KEEP YOUR FOCUS ON THE WORD

In addition to journaling, I have presented nine other methods in this chapter to consider to help you remember and record the things the Lord is teaching you through your personal quiet time. Try not to get overwhelmed with trying too many things at once, but focus instead on the object of our meditation, Jesus Christ, who is revealed to us in His Word. Be careful not to get so caught up in the method that your focus gets pulled away from the simple beauty of the Bible. A good study Bible with notes or devotions included is a good place to jump start your quiet time and rekindle your walk with Christ.

CHAPTER FIVE

WHEN YOUR WORLD TURNS UPSIDE DOWN

There are times in life when there is so much emotional upset, turmoil, and grief that it is difficult or impossible to steady our minds enough to read the Bible or even know how to pray. I am glad that God is gracious and compassionate, not grading us based on our spiritual performance. He sends people to help us in our time of need, holding up our arms when we are too weak to do so (as in Exodus 17:11–12), but sometimes we have to ask for help.

THE BLOODSTAINED BIBLE

LINDA'S STORY

"Nineteen-year-old female being transported to ER . . . status unresponsive."

Hardly the words I had expected to hear on a Sunday morning that had started out routinely as we headed to church to catch our early service. Our friends and neighbors, Mike and Linda, were running a few minutes behind us that day. Their daughter Amy and her friend were home from college visiting that weekend and were joining them for church. When we got to church, someone called to say that my friends had been in a bad accident. A truck had run a stop sign, hitting my friends' car and spinning it into a telephone pole. My husband and I rushed to the hospital, arriving before the ambulance got there. Although all four passengers were injured, it was Amy who was hurt the worst. Linda shared how she thought at first that her daughter was dying as she held her, propping her head up on her Bible as they waited for the first responders. In that moment Linda cried out to God to save Amy. "Hear my prayer, O Lord! And let my cry for help come to You" (Psalm 102:1, NASB).

Although she suffered a severe head injury and spent three days in ICU, hospitalized for a week altogether, Amy survived the accident. Linda recounts, "My heart was so devastated, so emotionally raw, that I couldn't concentrate. When I didn't have the strength to reach up to God, He leaned down to me. The Holy Spirit would bring Scriptures to my mind, and the verses I had highlighted in my Bible, shared with me by friends and family and written down on cards the previous year, ministered to me in the middle of the night as I sat by my daughter's bedside. Before having a regular quiet time, I couldn't remember where to find verses in my Bible."

Today, fourteen years later, Linda said her Bible still has Amy's blood stains on it. When I asked her why she didn't clean it off, she said, "Every time I see it, I am reminded how God answered my cry for help . . . I never want to forget that!"

~ Shared with permission
by Linda Sterling

AMY'S TESTIMONY FOLLOWING THE ACCIDENT

"Those next few months and years drastically changed my life, even parts of my personality. In regard to my quiet time with the Lord, the emotional part of my brain was one of the many parts that was injured. Previously, I had seen my dad reading his Bible and Daily Bread every morning, which was the example I followed starting years before this accident. I am thankful beyond words that I had the firm foundation because my world got rocked that day with ripple effects I still experience to this day. My world continued to swirl out of control, so I cried out to God in the "prayer closet" at my dorm. Let me restate that: I *tried* to cry or get angry or experience some emotion, but none came. My brain couldn't remember how. In hindsight, I believe God was protecting me from myself, but in the moment, I was at a loss. Over time, my emotions did reinvent themselves, albeit slightly altered from how they functioned before that day. During months and years of healing, I had the firm foundation of truth from years of quiet times with the Lord. Even when my emotions couldn't feel during those times, it was the continual habit of time with Him that kept me tethered to my healer!"

~ Shared with permission by Amy Bucholtz

As I was writing about Linda's story, I got a new text from her regarding her one-year-old great-nephew who is fighting cancer and is not doing well. This morning the family was hopeful, this afternoon, they are devastated as more cancer was found. Although she does not know how things will turn out with her nephew, Linda is confident that "God is good all the time." It is no wonder she feels that way about Him . . . she has walked closely with Him for years.

FOXHOLE CHRISTIANS

My husband has shared stories with me about guys who were foxhole Christians in Vietnam. When bullets were flying, some sent up desperate prayers begging for God's help; they promised to live their lives for God if He got them out of the situation alive. But often when the danger disappeared, so did their promises to commit their lives to Him. The truth is that we are in a battle in this world, and God wants to direct our steps, helping us to avoid the "booby traps and trip wires." He wants to dwell inside of us richly, preparing us for each day's challenges. He wants our walk to be fresh and real, daily drawing our spiritual strength from Him. If we seek God only when our back is against the wall, we miss the loving relationship, guidance, and strength He gives to prepare us for the battles ahead of us.

HOW CAN I POSSIBLY HANDLE *THIS*?

LANELLE'S STORY

I was only four when I remember telling God, "If this Jesus thing is for real, I want in on it!" About that same time, I remember standing in the living room of Granny and Pa's house and being scared for my parents to leave for a few hours. I was afraid they'd die in a car wreck, when I heard a voice inside of me say, "It's okay, that won't happen until you're an adult and can handle it."

Fast forward to when I was thirty-nine years old, Mom was sixty, and Dad was sixty-six, the day my childhood fears became a reality. It was around 5pm that fated day, June 14, 2013, when on their way to Branson for our extended family vacation, their Camry became their chariot into eternal paradise with God, Jesus, and loved ones.

I was packing and getting ready for the trip when the doorbell rang. When I saw the two troopers standing at the door, I ran away. Instinctively, I knew what had happened. God's still small voice had prepared me years ago. Still, I felt as if I could not breathe, and the Holy Spirit comforted and strengthened me to keep on breathing.

Although I can't say I see the purpose, I can see that He was preparing me for this. Weeks before their departure to heaven, my dad came to town to help us remodel a flip house. Brandon, my husband, wasn't going to join our sons, my parents, and me for that vacation in Branson unless we first put this house on the market. Dad came to the rescue and made a couple trips to town to help us. He told me, "Ya know, Nellie, I'm really glad I got this time doing everyday stuff with you. Your mom gets to all the time, but I really don't get to that much." I'm so glad he said that!

Mom and I had shopped together for clothes earlier that year. She always looked so beautiful. It was the last time we shopped like that together, and the first time I focused on her shopping rather than my own. Seems trivial, but looking back, it's not. We laughed and had a wonderful time together. A month or so after that, she said that you never know when you're going to get to have professional pictures again, so we might as well take advantage of the upcoming church directory photographs. She wore my shirt, sweater, and jewelry for that final professional picture. I insisted because I knew she wanted to. Again, this might seem trivial, but it's not. The hurt from *missed* opportunities for kindness between loved ones can become long-term pain and regret. On the other hand, those opportunities shared can well up fond memories that help us heal after loved ones depart from us, albeit temporarily. The promise of heaven makes even tragedy work for the good of those who love Him and are called according to His purpose.

Hours before they left this earth, I found two letters, one relating to my mom and one relating to my dad, that reiterated my answers to life questions. Later, I found Mom's handwritten note that said, "I'd like to be more like this, Lord," next to this verse in her Bible: "They do not fear bad news; they confidently trust the Lord to care for them" (Psalm 112:7, NLT).

I pray to be more like that too. And to accept that the Lord is sovereign; He giveth and He taketh away. Blessed be the name of the Lord. And thank God for sending Jesus Christ to take away our sins, and for the promise of heaven to make the purpose of this short time on earth lead to peace and eternal beauty. The end is a new beginning for those of us who have accepted "this Jesus thing." Rich and Rael Blubaugh (Mom & Dad) are happier and more fulfilled than ever, and we'll enjoy our time together some day, in the Lord's perfect timing.

~ Shared with permission by Lanelle Griffith

The thing I observed about the women whose stories I shared was the time they had spent with God in quiet time and prayer prior to the earth-shattering tragedies in their lives. They were grounded in their faith and better prepared to walk through suffering. These women had put their roots down deep in developing a personal love relationship with Jesus, and they understood that He is a good and loving God even through their tears and questioning.

"Developing the Christ-like habit of saying 'yes' to God, a habit nurtured in quiet time, develops a disposition in us that enables us to withstand greater 'loads' placed upon us, loads that perhaps right now we might crumble under."

~ Used by permission, Greg Herrick, www.Bible.org

Even if you are just a seeker or a new believer, rest assured that God will meet you just where you are. He loves you and will walk with you through your pain. "I [God] have certainly seen the oppression of My people in Egypt. I have heard their groans and have come down to rescue them" (Acts 7:34a, NLT).

As I thought about these three stories of trauma, I was reminded of a hymn we often sang at the little church I attended as a child. Titled "In Times Like These" by Ruth Kaye Jones, the song speaks of the tragic times in our lives when we desperately need a Savior. We all have times in life when we need someone to throw us a life preserver as the waves of life threaten to engulf us. In our most vulnerable times, Jesus can be our anchor, calming us and reassuring us in the midst of trouble.

The psalmist David could certainly relate to life spinning out of control. When the present seems unbearable, remember what God has done in the past.

PSALM 77 (NASB)

In the beginning of the chapter, David's raw emotions are evident:

- In the day of my trouble I sought the Lord . . .
- My soul refused to be comforted . . .
- When I sigh, my spirit grows faint . . .
- I am so troubled I cannot speak . . .
- Has God forgotten to be gracious?

Later in the chapter, after remembering God's works and pondering in his spirit, David says:

- Surely I will remember Your wonders of old . . .
- I will meditate on all Your work . . .
- Your way, O God, is holy . . .
- You are the God who works wonders . . .
- You have made known Your strength among the peoples . . .
- You led Your people like a flock . . .

Sometimes our world is rocked so hard that a quiet time comes crashing into our lives. Maybe it's in a hospital waiting room, a quiet chapel, reading a verse on a note or card, or the deafening silence in the middle of the night. Being too busy is no longer an issue as we desperately pray and seek comfort from God, pleading with Him to help us just survive as we grapple with the reality of the suffering we are walking through. Although a formal quiet time may not be possible, God's Spirit within you will comfort and strengthen you as He promises to be "our refuge and strength, a very present help in trouble" (Psalm 46:1, NASB).

CHAPTER SIX

RELATING TO GOD AS A LOVING FATHER

THE CASSETTE TAPE

A few weeks ago, as I was contemplating writing this chapter on our Heavenly Father's love and how that was modeled to me by my dad, I came across a small box simply labeled *tape.* It wasn't the first time I had seen it, as I had moved it from house to house and shifted it from place to place in my office for the past thirty-three years. My mom gave me the tape when my dad died suddenly during the Christmas season in 1983. Written on the top of the cassette tape were the words, *personal message to all my kids, recorded in three parts, 1972, 1979 and 1981. From Dad.* I had never been able to listen to it. I wasn't quite sure what would happen if I pressed the "play" button on that cassette, but I knew it would release an emotional floodgate, and I wasn't sure I was ready for that.

My dad had always communicated so much love to me. His countenance would light up when I came into the room, and his soft blue eyes were kind and loving. His first love, however, was for the Lord Jesus, and that overflowed to all three of his kids. I was devastated when my daddy passed away with a sudden heart attack at the age of seventy-three. That night I felt physical agony from the emotional grief as my mind had to absorb the reality I wanted so much to deny.

TELL ME WHAT A LOVING FATHER LOOKS LIKE

When I was in my early twenties, I was on the staff of Youth for Christ and had just left a meeting where my friend and I had shared with a group of teens how to have a personal relationship with the Heavenly Father by believing in His Son Jesus. Some of the kids were really struggling with the concept that God loved them unconditionally. When we were talking on the way home, I shared with my friend how sad that made me and how I even felt guilty about having had such a loving and godly father myself because there are so many people who didn't. My friend almost startled me with his response. "Stop right there! I know what you mean, but people like me who didn't have a good example of an earthly father need you to tell us what that looks like."

I never forgot that conversation, and I often wondered how I could share about my dad and my Heavenly Father in a humble way with people who have been deeply wounded, abused, or neglected by their father. Let me start by saying that for those of you who have been hurt, I am so sorry that the one person who should have modeled the love of Christ to you let you down.

The other day I talked with a young man who said, "I had a good dad. I was always taken to church, but somewhere along the line, I felt like I was just too much of a sinner and did not grasp the message about how much God accepted me. It wasn't until years later that I finally understood that, and when I received God's love for me, it changed everything!" My prayer is that whatever your background, you can learn the depth and width and height and length of the unconditional love God has for you. I pray also that you can receive by faith not only eternal salvation but also your adoption as His own beloved child. Sometimes, it may take the help of a Christian counselor to help you wade through the emotional hurt, but never forget this one thing. God wants you to draw close! "Draw near to God and He will draw near to you" (James 4:8a, HCSB). There is no motivational message or no amount of new ideas that can compare with the magnetic love of Christ drawing us into His presence.

I asked my friend recently to describe how having a father who was harsh and distant had affected her spiritual life. Without a blink, she said, "Oh, you just build a wall around your heart, because you have had so many disappointments and so much hurt. You become self-sufficient in order to survive. You push down your emotions and don't depend on anyone but yourself." But then, her face softened as she went on. "And then, about twenty years ago, when I was in my forties, someone came along and told me about Jesus and how much He loved me and wanted me to depend on Him! That was totally against everything I knew and believed. For me, learning to trust God is a process that has taken many years. When I read and learned more about the Bible and God's loving character, I was able to grow closer to Him."

BACK TO THE TAPE

My father started out his audio message to us kids by saying, "If I could just have had one more talk with my dad . . . " He had a close relationship with his dad, and it ended way too soon. What a common wish for any of us that grieve! After saying a few personal things to my brother, sister, and I, he went on to share about his life, as if he were having that one last talk with us. So I want to pass on to you some of the things this man of God recorded, as I know in my heart he would want to share it with you too!

Dad was so grateful that despite some very hard times living through the depression, surviving a train wreck at age nineteen that resulted in chronic back pain, and other life trials, he felt like his life was wonderful due to his faith, hope, and trust in Christ. He loved his family and wanted God's best for each one of us. It was obvious through his words that as he aged, the important things about life were becoming clearer to him. "Now we see things imperfectly, like puzzling reflections in a mirror, but then we will see everything with perfect clarity. All that I know now is partial and incomplete, but then I will know everything completely, just as God now knows me completely" (1 Cor. 13:12, NLT).

Dad spoke of all of us who believe in Christ being together again someday, complete as a family. He said how important and fragile that life is, and then quoted 2 Corinthians 3:2 (KJV): "Ye are our epistle written in our hearts, known and read of all men." It took a moment to recognize this verse from the old King James Version, but then I realized that this was my favorite verse, which is the theme of my website, *Letters Written on Our Hearts*. Wow, of all the verses he could have used, he used my favorite (although I don't remember him ever telling me about this verse)! Once again, my heart was weaved together with his, not so much as father and daughter, but as fellow heirs of Christ. He went on to talk about the importance of giving back to God, in the form of tithes, but emphasized that "all He really wants is you. It matters to Him about you!" He made the analogy of the Hallmark theme, caring enough to send the very best, saying God cared enough to send His very best to us, in the form of His Son.

Dad told of a trip he made to see one of his cousins, whose son was in prison. Dad wanted to visit, but his cousin said very few visitors were allowed. Still, Dad was determined and talked the warden into letting him in. He spoke of the hour-long visit that ended with Dad asking the young man if he could pray with him, which they did. Dad wanted everyone to know how much God loved them, despite their circumstances. Later he learned his cousin's son got out of prison, got a job, and returned to his young family.

If I could think of one characteristic that I loved about my father, it would be his loving-kindness to me. Recently, my son sent me a website that had a beautiful video presentation about the Father's love from the ministry of Barry Adams, which you can view at FathersLoveLetter.com.

BARRY'S STORY

(in his own words relating to a men's retreat he attended in 1998)

Near the end of the weekend, the speaker, Jack Winter, asked if I had wanted to be prayed for to receive a deeper revelation of the Father's love for me. As Jack prayed for me, I began to feel all the pain and disappointment of a little boy just wanting to be loved. In contrast to the emptiness, I also felt the incredible warmth of God the Father wrapping His arms around me. Wave upon wave of the love of God began to touch the deepest places in my heart that had been so wounded and discouraged as a child. While I had always had a theological understanding of God as my Father, this was the first time that I had such a powerful encounter with God that impacted my body, soul, and spirit. After encountering God in such a powerful way, I began to see the Father's love everywhere I looked in the Bible. It was like the "lights had been turned on," and I could see the theme of the Father heart of God throughout the entire Bible. I can remember the day that I asked God to help me to better comprehend His love in light of all of the Scriptures that I was now seeing throughout the Bible. In my heart, I immediately heard a still small voice say . . . *"If you put the Scriptures in the right order, they will form a love letter."*

WHAT IS FATHER'S LOVE LETTER?

Father's Love Letter is a compilation of Bible verses from both the Old & New Testaments that are presented in the form of a love letter from God to you.

Each line in the Father's Love Letter message is paraphrased, which means we have taken each Scripture's overall message and summarized it as a single phrase to best express its meaning.

FATHER'S LOVE LETTER

AN INTIMATE MESSAGE FROM GOD TO YOU . . .

My Child,

You may not know me, but I know everything about you.

Psalm 139:1

I know when you sit down and when you rise up.

Psalm 139:2

I am familiar with all your ways.

Psalm 139:3

Even the very hairs on your head are numbered.

Matthew 10:29–31

For you were made in my image.

Genesis 1:27

In me you live and move and have your being.

Acts 17:28

For you are my offspring.

Acts 17:28

I knew you even before you were conceived.

Jeremiah 1:4–5

I chose you when I planned creation.

Ephesians 1:11–12

You were not a mistake, for all your days are written in my book.

Psalm 139:15–16

I determined the exact time of your birth and where you would live.

Acts 17:26

You are fearfully and wonderfully made.

Psalm 139:14

I knit you together in your mother's womb.

Psalm 139:13

And brought you forth on the day you were born.

Psalm 71:6

I have been misrepresented by those who don't know me.

John 8:41–44

I am not distant and angry, but am the complete expression of love.

1 John 4:16

And it is my desire to lavish my love on you.

1 John 3:1

Simply because you are my child and I am your Father.

1 John 3:1

I offer you more than your earthly father ever could.

Matthew 7:11

For I am the perfect father.

Matthew 5:48

Every good gift that you receive comes from my hand.

James 1:17

For I am your provider and I meet all your needs.

Matthew 6:31–33

My plan for your future has always been filled with hope.

Jeremiah 29:11

Because I love you with an everlasting love.

Jeremiah 31:3

My thoughts toward you are countless as the sand on the seashore.

Psalm 139:17–18

And I rejoice over you with singing.

Zephaniah 3:17

I will never stop doing good to you.

Jeremiah 32:40

For you are my treasured possession.

Exodus 19:5

I desire to establish you with all my heart and all my soul.

Jeremiah 32:41

And I want to show you great and marvelous things.

Jeremiah 33:3

If you seek me with all your heart, you will find me.

Deuteronomy 4:29

Delight in me and I will give you the desires of your heart.

Psalm 37:4

For it is I who gave you those desires.

Philippians 2:13

I am able to do more for you than you could possibly imagine.

Ephesians 3:20

For I am your greatest encourager.

2 Thessalonians 2:16–17

I am also the Father who comforts you in all your troubles.

2 Corinthians 1:3–4

When you are brokenhearted, I am close to you.

Psalm 34:18

As a shepherd carries a lamb, I have carried you close to
my heart.

Isaiah 40:11

One day I will wipe away every tear from your eyes.

Revelation 21:3–4

And I'll take away all the pain you have suffered on this earth.

Revelation 21:3–4

I am your Father, and I love you even as I love my son, Jesus.

John 17:23

For in Jesus, my love for you is revealed.

John 17:26

He is the exact representation of my being.

Hebrews 1:3

He came to demonstrate that I am for you, not against you.

Romans 8:31

And to tell you that I am not counting your sins.

2 Corinthians 5:18–19

Jesus died so that you and I could be reconciled.

2 Corinthians 5:18–19

His death was the ultimate expression of my love
for you.

1 John 4:10

I gave up everything I loved that I might gain your love.

Romans 8:31–32

If you receive the gift of my son Jesus, you receive me.

1 John 2:23

And nothing will ever separate you from my love again.

Romans 8:38–39

Come home and I'll throw the biggest party
heaven has ever seen.

Luke 15:7

I have always been Father, and will always be Father.

Ephesians 3:14–15

My question is . . . Will you be my child?

John 1:12–13

I am waiting for you.

Luke 15:11–32

Love, Your Dad

Almighty God

Father's Love Letter used by permission
@1999 Father Heart Communications
FathersLoveLetter.com

CHAPTER SEVEN

I'M SICK AND TIRED!

HEALTH PROBLEMS

Health problems, often accompanied by chronic pain, can take their toll on a person's mind, will, and emotions, which also affects a person's relationship with God. My friend Kathy Guzzo has a serious, debilitating, and painful condition that she has battled for years. Recently, I asked her if having chronic pain affects a person's relationship with Christ, even causing them at times to feel like leaving their first love (God). Surprisingly, she answered back with a resounding yes, because it had happened to her. Although Kathy is a gracious and sweet woman who is always giving to others, it was obvious that my question had touched a chord with her. Thankfully, she was willing to share part of her journey with my readers.

Kathy started by saying that when most people think of quiet time, they picture someone in the early morning sitting in a quiet place with a warm drink, a journal, and a Bible. However, when health issues are added, the picture is blurred and the pieces need to be put together differently.

HONEST NEGATIVE REACTIONS THAT CAN
STEAL OUR JOY AND TRUST IN THE LORD

- In the midst of appointments, medical tests, diagnosis, pain, fatigue, and other symptoms, we as humans want to get angry and blame someone for our discomfort, and so we lash out at God. After all, He created us and allows us to be in this condition. In the same way that we often take it out on those closest to us because we know they love us unconditionally, the same is true of our response to God.

- Isolating ourselves from other believers and/or family can compound the problem as we draw within and away from our support system.

- Escaping from reality by filling our mind with too much food, television, online games, or social media is a temptation, as it is often easier to get lost in reality shows or stories than to deal with our own reality drama!

- Becoming obsessed with the illness, reading everything available, trying different treatments or diets, and talking obsessively about it can take over our lives. Our illness can easily become our god if we allow it.

I'm not sure why, but guilt plays a huge part in the life of a person with a chronic illness. So, if they miss a day or two of having a quiet time, the guilt sets in, making it harder to get back to the time set aside with God. I think that's true of all of us, so here are some suggestions that can help.

FIVE PRACTICAL SUGGESTIONS FOR
HAVING A MEANINGFUL QUIET TIME WHILE
LIVING WITH A CHRONIC ILLNESS

1. I must give myself permission to be creative with my quiet time and realize that doesn't look the same to all people. The time of day, the length of time, even the place isn't nearly as important as the heart to seek Him. For most people with chronic illness, no two days are alike. One day I may wake feeling refreshed and ready for the picture-perfect quiet time, but the next day I may be in pain or exhausted from lack of sleep and need a couple hours to even get going. Then on the days when there are doctor appointments, medical tests, phone calls to insurance companies, etc., I need to prioritize and rearrange my schedule.

2. If I'm trying to get back into the routine of having a quiet time, I need to remember it's okay to start small. When I do sit for a quiet time, it can be hard to pray, focus on His Word, and/or hear His voice, because my symptoms, especially on what is known as the bad days, are ever present. Just as my mouth feels refreshed after one to two minutes of brushing my teeth, my soul can feel refreshed after reading one Bible verse, one devotional, even one minute of prayer.

3. Writing in my gratitude journal must be done daily. Sometimes there are days, yes, even weeks, when I don't really feel up to spending quality time with the Lord, but I can always find at least one thing each day to be grateful for. By

writing them down, I'm acknowledging God's goodness in my life, and rereading the list each day helps my heart and mind to focus on Him and all He's done for me.

4. I will accept that it's okay to have a quiet time even if my attitude isn't one of praise and gratefulness. When sitting to soak in His love, it's easier to pour out my problems, my questions, and my emotions since they are ever present and seem to take center stage in my life. God can handle my frustrations, anger, questions, and feelings of insecurity. In fact, since He knows everything about me, He's the perfect One to vent to.

5. I can't get discouraged or give up on a having a special time with God. As life changes, so will my quiet time, but I have the assurance that wherever and whenever I choose to meet with Him, He'll be there waiting. Life with a chronic illness is one day at a time, which is exactly how He desires us to live.

~ Used by permission - Kathy Guzzo

CAREGIVERS

During more than twenty years of working as an eldercare case manager in a job I dearly loved, I spent a lot of time assessing the needs of disabled or elderly people and helping families come up with a plan of care for them. This process often brought to attention the often-overlooked needs of the caregivers, who sometimes needed to be included in the care plan themselves. Many times the caregivers would get serious health issues or even die before the primary patients, as they had neglected to take care of themselves. I helped to take care of my sweet mother for many years, and she was almost ninety-eight years old when she passed away. The year before she died, I found myself in the hospital four times, and as I look back, I see how the stress of caregiving took its toll on me. I believe the information given earlier in this chapter is applicable to caregivers as it relates to quiet time. If you are a caregiver for one or more people, I would encourage you to ask for help from your family members, church, or community programs so that you can find time to recharge and take care of yourself. In the long run, you will be doing your family member or friend a favor if you don't run yourself into the ground.

COMPASSION FATIGUE

I remember the day I first heard about compassion fatigue. I was actually searching the web to learn about job burnout (that's another book), and compassion fatigue popped up. It was a multiple choice test, and my score was off the chart. The disclaimer said that it was not an official measurement, but it also suggested that if we fell within a certain range, we might want to get some professional help. *Whap.* I felt like someone had hit me upside the head! I was used to being the helper, not the helpee. However, that was the day I called in for a counseling referral. I was at the end of the line and I needed help figuring out how I got to this place, and how to get back to a balanced life.

Somewhere along the line, I had gotten swallowed up in ministry activities and work, running faster and faster with no boundaries. My family was fading away in the background, as was my quiet time in God's presence. I remember telling the counselor confidently that I was the kind of person who performed at 110 percent. "Really?" she said. "Have you ever considered 100 or maybe even 90 percent?" I looked at her dumbfounded because, no, I had never considered that, thinking to myself, "You can do that? Really?"

Over the next few weeks, I realized that I was depressed and angry and way beyond overloaded. I began a process of being kinder to myself, setting healthy boundaries with others, and eventually leaving a job that was sucking the life out of me. Undoing a lifetime of bad habits was a process, but with God's gentle guidance and direction, I remembered how to walk with Him again. Instead of grabbing a spiritual snack, I sat with His Word, pondering and meditating and listening for His still small voice within my spirit. I remember the day I was taking a walk and I felt the sun shining down on me. It was more than the warmth of the sun that made me smile once again. It was the warmth of the Son who had somehow shown me the way back home.

GENERAL FATIGUE

When you've asked someone how they are feeling, has anyone ever responded with "Rested! I feel so rested and refreshed!" There are so many people who are just plain exhausted and so many reasons for it. Being tired is bound to affect our spiritual condition, as we simply don't have the energy or physical stamina to fight off sleepiness. My friend's daughter has three little children under the age of two, and she certainly can relate to not getting much sleep these days. Although sometimes the things surrounding fatigue are unavoidable, there are a few things we can do to get more rest and have the energy to give God our best.

Make your bedroom a soothing quiet place, uncluttered and inviting. Clean sheets and a hot shower or bath before bedtime can be helpful.

Begin to wind down the electronic devices the hour before you go to bed. Recharge your phone at a distance from your bed and turn off notifications that aren't absolutely needed.

Reassess eating habits with a dietician, doctor, or personal trainer to determine if changes are needed in your diet or daily exercise to increase energy levels.

Dawson Trotman of the Navigators knew that the last dominant conscious thought in the human mind at the end of the day would inevitably simmer in the subconscious during sleep and help shape the attitude and personality of the heart. And he was right. If you want to hide God's Word in your heart (Psalm 119:11), go to sleep while meditating on a verse of Scripture (Read Joshua 1:8 and Psalm 1:2, 63:6, 77:6, 119:97). It seeps into your subconscious mind and helps shape your soul. You'll sleep better and wake up the next morning more refreshed.

FAN THE FLAMES

My husband is quite the fire bug. He told me of a time spent camping with some guys when they built a raging campfire. During the night it began to rain hard, and when morning came, the lack of fuel and oxygen had put the fire out. Shivering from the cool morning air, Steve found a stick and started stirring the wet mushy ashes when he noticed a few stray coals. He put them all together in one place, pushed some stray branches together, and soon the fire began to flicker once again, providing warmth and heat for cooking their breakfast.

Sometimes our lives can feel like those coals buried in the ashes. If we can push past our feelings to draw close to God, it not only helps us but can also spark an ember that may ignite fresh hope and faith in others as we look past our own pain and come alongside others who are hurting. God has gifted each of us in unique ways and will give us the power and strength to minister His grace and love to others. "This is why I remind you to fan into flames the spiritual gift God gave you when I laid my hands on you" (2 Tim. 1:6, NLT). Although we can fan the flames, it is the Holy Spirit who is the originator of the fire that burns in our soul. It's not by trying harder to be a better Christian but by opening the door of our hearts that He is knocking on that we enter His rest, drawing strength in time of need. It is only one day at a time that He asks, and He promises strength for today and hope for tomorrow. "And endurance develops strength of character, and character strengthens our confident hope of salvation" (Rom. 5:4, NLT).

CHAPTER EIGHT

THE HIGH COST OF UNFORGIVENESS

I CAN'T SEEM TO FORGIVE!

 I have often found myself sincerely wanting to have a meaningful time in my devotions. My Bible is open, my journal nearby, and my desire to be spiritually fed is high. I am a seeker on these days, seeking an encounter with my very personal God. Yet something is wrong. If I sit quietly long enough, I become keenly aware of the unrest in my soul. Deeper reflection reveals a root of bitterness that has crept into the garden of my heart. At that point, there are certain verses I honestly don't want to read right then, such as "And be kind and compassionate to one another, forgiving one another, just as God also forgave you in Christ." (Eph. 4:32, HCSB). Even though I know the conviction of the Holy Spirit comes to me cloaked with loving-kindness and gentle admonition, my strong will and stubborn heart refuse to release that unforgiveness to God, allowing Him to deal with the person who has wronged me. The roadblock of that unforgiveness hampers my

intimacy with God and detours my efforts to enter into His presence. I do not have a thankful heart, so how can I enter into His gates with thanksgiving and into His courts with praise? I go ahead and read the verses before me. I lay my request before the Lord in prayer. I ask Him, "What does love look like when I've been repeatedly hurt?" That question hangs in the air, and my quiet time with the Lord leaves me spiritually hungry and longing for so much more.

I have a friend, John, in my Sunday school class who began to study 1 Corinthians 13 about ten years ago. He found the chapter so fascinating and convicting, a kaleidoscope of insights and truth dealing with the most important element of the Christian life—love. He decided to read it every day. Something happened to John. His wife commented that he seemed to mellow, to soften and demonstrate love to her and others around him in noticeable ways. As he watched me struggle with my issues, he would often gently share with me his own journey through this powerful chapter and remind me of the importance to love others, especially those who had wronged me. One of the verses, 1 Corinthians 13:5b (NASB) says love "does not keep a record of wrongs." I've read this verse dozens of times over the years, yet I still found myself defensive, saying, "Yes, but in the situation that *I'm* in, what does love look like?" I was so busy asking that question, that I wasn't meditating on those verses and asking the Holy Spirit to help me understand them and to empower me to apply them. I was beginning to realize, though, that in order to come to grips with how to forgive the people who had wronged me, I had to crash headlong into the issue of love.

My unforgiveness toward different people had caused bitter roots to wrap so tightly around my heart that the bitterness choked out all else. Its poison spilled into the ears of my friends and family, and even strangers. My venting had led to ranting that led to deep-seated anger and bitterness. The truth was, I had been wounded, and the wounds would not heal. I could justify my response for hours, going over and over the details. Then I would get hurt again, which would trigger old memories, and yet another root of bitterness would entangle itself around my heart. No matter how hard I tried, I could not, or would not, let go and forgive, and it was affecting my quiet time, my relationship with family and friends, and my ministry. I needed God to break this toxic stronghold before it consumed me.

My breakthrough began one night when I was praying the 23rd Psalm back to God. I got to verse five where it said, "you prepare a table before me in the presence of my enemies," and I stopped to ponder the meaning of that. Who are my enemies? Was it a co-worker, a family member, a friend, or the stranger who was rude to me in the checkout line? Or maybe it was a real enemy who threatened me or my family.

One night a few weeks later, I had an unexpected wake-up call from the Lord. This night, He decided to answer the recurring question I had wrestled with for years. As I got up and walked by the bookshelf in my office, I randomly picked up this very old book I had gotten at a family estate sale about seven years ago. The title of this old classic was *The Greatest Thing in the World* written in 1890 by Henry Drummond. It had been a gift to my great uncle. I had no idea that the book was all about 1 Corinthians 13. With each sentence I read, I looked square into the face of love and saw what it did and didn't look like. I began to realize that my response to offenses or perceived offenses had led to a bitter root, one that took hold in my heart and spirit. My own "ill-temper," as the old classic said, was a sin that could damage my testimony and could very well be worse than the sins of those who had hurt me. As I confessed the sins of anger and unforgiveness to my loving Heavenly Father, I felt free of the stronghold that had held me captive so long. When I saw the movie *War Room,* it became clear that I had been taking on a battle that should have been given to the Lord, as only He can convict of sin and win over people's hearts. I can only be responsible to love as He loved.

"Souls are made sweet not by taking acid fluids out but by putting something in—a great Love, a new Spirit, the Spirit of Christ."

~ *The Greatest Thing in the World* by Henry Drummond

I realized now why my friend John continued to nudge me to love like Christ loved. I still needed to set healthy boundaries in my relationships and even sought professional counseling to sort through my emotions. But the freedom that came when I was able to forgive was liberating. I could approach the Lord with a clear conscience and receive from Him the spiritual food He had set before me on that table. I was able to "taste and see" that He is good, and my own lack of forgiveness was no longer a closed, wounded heart but instead a heart set free to seek God in a new and powerful way.

Sara Horn, in her book, *How Can I Possibly Forgive* (pg. 69), says, "When we can own up to what's holding us captive, whatever it is, we open the door for God to work and change us into the women he desires us to be." As you consider this, are you being held captive by unforgiveness? Is there someone you need to forgive? Are you willing to release that person to God and open up your heart to forgive them? When you forgive others as you have been forgiven, you will then be able to experience freedom, joy, and intimate fellowship in your quiet times with the Lord.

I'VE DONE TOO MUCH TO BE FORGIVEN

For the past twenty years, my husband and I have worked with a Christian ministry for veterans and their families. When we have shared the good news of the Bible with them about God's free gift of forgiveness, we often hear the same thing: "Oh, but I've done too much to be forgiven!"

There was a Vietnam veteran that I met when he was in our town for a seven-week in-patient treatment program at the VA Medical Center. He was actively involved in mining ships during the war. The death and destruction of war left him with a wounded heart. He came home feeling he needed forgiveness for a number of things he did while serving in the military. Some were things that he was ordered to do by his commanding officers, and others were personal sins. Both resulted in moral wounds of the soul that needed a spiritual healing. He went to his priest to ask for forgiveness, but the priest told him he had done too much to be forgiven. This only confirmed his worst fears about himself, and so he gave up trying to do the right thing and in his words "proceeded to raise hell for the next thirty years."

I have to admit I was a little intimidated by this tall rough biker guy sitting next to me at the Point Man ministry dinner we had invited him to attend. It was the last night he would be there because he was due to graduate from the program a few days later. That night, my husband gifted him with a dog tag with the word "forgiven" punched out of the metal, explaining that we've all done too much to be forgiven. My husband explained that when our commanding officer says something to us, we don't argue but respond with an immediate "yes, sir!" In the same way, in a spiritual sense, God is our commanding officer. He has said in Romans 5:8 HCSB, "But God proves His own love for us in that while we were still sinners, Christ died for us!" So when Christ says, "Son, you are forgiven," we need not argue that we've done too much to be forgiven, but only say "Yes, Sir, I believe." When our veteran friend heard the good news of the gospel at the Point Man meeting that night, he said, "I've come full circle! Once I thought I was forgiven, then I thought I couldn't be forgiven, and now I know I *am* forgiven."

UNFORGIVENESS TOWARD GOD

Have you ever felt like God is the one you can't forgive for allowing certain things to happen to you? Maybe you have had more than your share of suffering, loss, or abuse. Some veterans have expressed they feel God went AWOL (absent without leave) at the moment they needed Him the most. Once our pastor was addressing the issue of questioning God about why bad things happen. I remember him saying that there is nothing wrong with asking God why with hands lifted to heaven, but we should be careful not to defiantly shake our fist heavenward. There are no easy answers to the question of why God allows suffering to happen to us, but I believe the Lord would have us cry out to Him for help and comfort and wisdom during these times.

I was speaking with a young wife recently who had been deeply hurt. She hesitantly confessed that she sometimes became angry at God for allowing her to be hurt despite all of her attempts to do everything right, while the offending person in her life seemed to get off easy. If this is your struggle:

Pour out your heart and your feelings to God. "Arise, cry aloud in the night at the beginning of the night watches; Pour out your heart like water before the presence of the Lord" (Lam.2:19a, NASB).

Entrust yourself to Him who judges justly (1 Peter 2:21–23). Trust the character of God, His loving-kindness, His mercy, and His justice.

One of the fruits of the Holy Spirit is patience . . . pray for this fruit to be evident in your life as you lay down the issue that is causing your anger toward God and wait for Him to work. It may be days, weeks, or years. Stand firm and keep trusting.

When tempted not to forgive God, I have a word for you. In spite of being overwhelmed by your circumstances and your feelings, I ask that you pause and just remember. Remember His blessings. Remember how much He loves you. Remember how much you (and all people) need forgiveness from Him and how He has saved you. Remember He created you for a unique purpose. Remember that He is the potter and you are the clay. Remember this is our temporary home and heaven awaits. And as you remember, enter His rest.

CHAPTER NINE

DUSTY GOLD!

One of the world's most successful treasure hunters spent many years searching for a 17th century shipwreck, suffering one setback after another—including the death of his son. The daughter of the treasure hunter told how, every day, he would say, "Today is the day we're going to hit gold; we're getting so close!" But then day after day of diving would yield nothing, and he'd say, "That's all right, we'll find it tomorrow." And the next day he'd declare again, "Today is the day." The treasure hunter's discovery came after many years of searching that nearly bankrupted him before he finally located the sunken ship in 1985. Even though they recovered more than $450 million in gold, jewels, and other artifacts, the family heirs revealed on a television documentary that there may be an additional quarter-million dollars still buried at sea. Imagine that! A treasure sitting on the bottom of the ocean since the 17th century that was dismissed and forgotten by most, now brought to the surface and repurposed for a new use.

I admire this treasure hunter's tenacity and determination never to give up despite tremendous odds. I wonder what would happen if we could see the Bible as having spiritual treasures and approach our time with the Bible expectantly day after day, saying, "Today is the day I am going to find it!" When speaking of the good news of the gospel, Peter writes the following: "It is all so wonderful that even the angels are eagerly watching these things happen" (1 Peter 1:12b, NLT).

What if the treasure was hidden right there beside us in the dusty Bible on the shelf, and God through His Holy Spirit was ready to reveal to you a personal discovery that not only related to your life but would clarify your life's purpose? What if sharing that valuable jewel of a verse gave hope to someone else whose faith was wearing thin? What if it led them to experience a personal relationship with Christ that affected their spouse, kids, and family, breaking a generation of faithlessness? What if?

SPELUNKING

One of my husband's hobbies is spelunking, or caving, with his friend Rick. I still cringe when my three adult sons and their dad sit around the table and tell caving stories. It's a good thing this mamma didn't know then about the steep drop-offs and slippery slopes they were climbing around on underground until well after the trip was over! Those caving trips required a lot of work as they gathered together all of the equipment needed for their fun adventure. There are some rules for caving that can teach us some things as we seek to dive deeper into the Word of God.

RICK'S CAVING RULES

Caving, also known as spelunking or potholing in the UK, is an adventurous sport for those explorers drawn to search below the Earth's surface for hidden beauty or treasures. It is important to recognize the dangers involved in going caving alone: steep descents, slippery surfaces, cold temperatures, and the risk of flooding.

1. Never Cave Alone!

It is important not to go caving alone due to the risk of getting injured without having someone there to help you. The National Speleological Society (NSS) recommends caving in groups of four or five. That way, the group is not so big that movement is impeded, and a team of two or three can be sent for help in case of an emergency, while another stays with the injured party.

Lesson to be learned:

The Bible speaks of having two or three gathered together and that God will be present with them. When we start to falter or stumble in our faith, the tendency is for us to isolate and instead of leaning on our family of fellow believers, we often fight our battles alone. In order to be building one another up, we need our brothers and sisters in Christ to remind us that God is there for us! "He comforts us in all our troubles so that we can comfort others. When they are troubled, we will be able to give them the same comfort God has given us" (2 Cor. 1:4, NLT).

2. Prepare ahead

Do your homework ahead of the trip and make sure you have the training to know what to expect. Always let someone know where you are going and when you plan to be back. By learning about the dangers of caving from those who have gone before, the chances are greater that the experience will be an adventure and not an unfortunate tragedy.

Lesson to be learned:

Just as an athletic endeavor like caving requires preparation and training, so does the Christian need training to know how to grow as a believer. "Solid food is for those who are mature, who through training have the skill to recognize the difference between right and wrong" (Hebrews 5:14, NLT). Solid Bible teaching and discipleship classes can help equip believers to have a faith that remains strong when the storms of life threaten to weaken it. Discipleship or mentoring programs, Christian life coaching, online classes, or adult classes at church can provide helpful training to equip us to better serve Christ.

3. Have the right equipment

Head gear: Moving through tight spaces, you're likely to bump your head a few times. Always wearing a protective hat will guard against concussions and injury.

Knee and elbow pads: Your knees will thank you as you'll probably spend considerable time crawling.

Gloves: That's for the cave, not you. The oils on your hands can kill cave formations, and it's always good to follow good conservation practices.

Boots: Avoid wearing tennis shoes unless you want to skate down a slippery slope! If you go into a cave with streams, keep an eye on the weather to avoid flooding in the cave. The NSS has a full list of basic and optional equipment that's worth checking before your next expedition.

Misc.: Have three independent sources of light and extra batteries, a first aid kit, food, and water.

Lesson to be learned:

We face many conflicts each day, and battles rage around the world. The unseen spiritual battle for our souls is one that can wound our faith in Christ, so it is vital that we have the right spiritual gear to protect our minds and hearts from the enemy's attack. My husband and his veteran friends often speak of the different terms to describe combat fatigue; shell shock in WWI, battle fatigue in WWII, PTSD in Vietnam, and Soldier's Heart in the Civil War. We believers can suffer from battle fatigue in the spiritual realm. "Therefore, put on every piece of God's armor so you will be able to resist the enemy in the time of evil. Then after the battle, you will still be standing firm" (Eph. 6:13, NLT).

If you think about it, each piece of the armor of God represents a name of Christ, and as we put on the armor, we put on Christ Himself. How do we do this? The answer is in verse 18 that tells us to pray in the Spirit at all times and on every occasion. We can pray, asking God to clothe us with His armor, and then after the battle, we will still be standing firm, allowing Him to do the fighting. Instead of the enemy seeing us, he sees Christ. The belt of truth will keep us on level ground; the breastplate of righteousness will protect our hearts; the good news of the gospel as our shoes gives us sure footing and protects us from stumbling; the shield of faith stops the fiery arrows of the devil; the helmet of salvation protects our minds; and the sword of the Spirit is the Word of God, which is our foundation.

THE TREASURE I ACCIDENTALLY FOUND!

One day about twenty years ago, I was casually reading my Bible and turned to Job chapter 28. I was fascinated by what I found there.

Job speaks of miners going underground to find beautiful jewels of copper, lapis lazuli (blue sapphire), coral, jasper, rubies, peridot (an apple green stone), crystal, onyx, jade, opal, pearls, silver, and gold! People go about their business above ground, unaware of the treasures below. In the middle of my imagining what all those bedazzled stones looked like, the passage took an unexpected turn. It wasn't the precious jewels that couldn't be found by people, but something else. The perplexing question was posed: "But do people know where to find wisdom? Where can they find understanding? It is hidden from the eyes of all humanity. Even the sharp-eyed birds in the sky cannot discover it" (Job 28:20–21, NLT). The Bible doesn't leave those two questions unanswered, as you can see in verse 28. The treasure for me in this chapter was the things I learned about wisdom and understanding and how it paralleled that of those underground prospectors.

FOUR OBSERVATIONS AND APPLICATIONS FROM JOB 28

People above ground are oblivious to the treasure hunt going on right beneath their feet. Sometimes people don't want to go where the treasures are. It may be too risky, too scary, or too much work. We forget that in order to find the gems, we have to search for them because they are hidden. And so we scurry about, often missing out on gold nuggets so close we could reach out and touch them if only we would try.

On his own strength, man can do many things. The lure of wealth motivates men to do superhuman feats, sinking mine shafts, descending on ropes swinging back and forth (think the curse of Oak Island!), tearing apart flinty rocks to cut in tunnels, damming up springs, and bringing to light hidden treasures. However, in all his feats, he cannot get true wisdom and understanding without God, as He alone knows the way.

People often seek value and worth in the things of this world rather than seeing the value and worth of what God offers us. If we could refocus on what is really important, how would our goals change? Repurposing when it comes to how we spend our time can lead us to the real purpose for which we were designed!

We grope around in darkness, forgetting our source of light and that, in Christ, there is no darkness. "You must pay close attention to what they [the prophets] wrote, for their words are like a lamp shining in a dark place—until the Day dawns, and Christ the Morning Star shines in your hearts" (2 Peter 1:19b, NLT).

The real treasure is Christ living in our hearts. "We now have this light shining in our hearts, but we ourselves are like fragile clay jars containing this great treasure. This makes it clear that our great power is from God, not from ourselves" (2 Cor. 4:7, NLT). What a relief to know that God understands our weakness; He will repurpose and rebuild and restore as we daily open our hearts to Him.

Just as there are hurdles to overcome and great hardship to mine for underground treasures, so we have trials here on earth. How God can give us joy when there is often overwhelming grief and sadness is a mystery. Sometimes it's just trusting and being encouraged by His Word. "So be truly glad. There is wonderful joy ahead, even though you have to endure many trials for a little while. These trials will show that your faith is genuine. It is being tested as fire tests and purifies gold—though your faith is far more precious than mere gold" (1 Peter 1:6–7b, NLT). No wonder the angels are eagerly watching as God's plan for all mankind unfolds . . . as God's plan for you unfolds!

CHAPTER TEN

REPURPOSED FAITH – REKINDLED GRACE

If you are in a place where your faith is worn, lacking purpose, weak, or small, don't lose heart. The good news is that God is in the business of taking ordinary people with tiny little faith the size of a mustard seed (Matt. 17:20) and making their faith extraordinary. The power of the Spirit of God within us can strengthen us during periods of suffering, waiting, and brokenness, and can give us joy in the midst of sorrow. God is in the business of refreshing your heart, renewing your strength, and restoring your faith as you draw close to Him and allow the power of His love to lead you into greater intimacy with Him.

Jesus has extended an invitation to believe in Him and to walk in His ways. Repurposed faith is faith in action. In following Him, we step into His purpose for us and all mankind, to know Him and the power of His resurrection through the forgiveness of our sins. As you seek to know Christ better, you may have trouble understanding the Bible, but you can pray and ask the Lord to make it clear to you. "Then he opened their minds to understand the Scriptures" (Luke 24:45, HCSB).

For those of us who have been Christians for many years, it takes concentrated effort to pause and consider the meaning of Bible verses we have heard so often that we become immune to their meaning and application to our lives. Becoming haphazard or downright lazy when it comes to eating our daily spiritual food, we slowly drift away, cut off from our power source and wondering what happened to the fire that once burned in our souls. Our pride does not want to admit that we have become lukewarm, and so we cover up the root issue by running faster and harder in good church activities or trying harder to be a good Christian, always wondering if there is not a greater purpose and calling. Others go to the other extreme, withdrawing and drifting away from the Lord, weary in heart or burned out. The enemy would have us feel like the gap between us and God is too great, but the truth is that just as when we first came to Christ with the simple faith and trust of a child, so re-connecting that faith to the power source is one prayer away. "Draw near to God and He will draw near to you" (James 4:8a, NASB). Despite any negative messages you have been told, the truth found in the Bible says some pretty amazing things about you.

REKINDLED GRACE

If you are a believer who desires a deeper walk with Christ, remember that "your life is hidden with Christ in God" (Col. 3:3b NASB). Sometimes we can lose heart and lose hope when things or relationships we used to feel confidently in control of have crashed and burned along with our dreams for the future. Although dreams can die, they can also be reborn, repurposed for His plan as we re-lease control, regain trust, and ask God to reveal Himself and His purpose to us. "For I know the plans I have for you, says the Lord. They are plans for good and not for disaster, to give you a future and a hope" (Jeremiah 29:11, NLT). Consider what He says about you and your purpose. "I cry out to God Most High, to God who will fulfill His purpose for me" (Psalm 57:2, NLT).

- You are loved (John 3:16).

- You are called (2 Peter 1:3).

- You are gifted (Romans 12:6).

- You are redeemed (Psalm 107:2).

- You are a new creation (2 Corinthians 5:17).

- You are His ambassador (2 Corinthians 5:20).

- You are cleansed from sin (Psalm 51:2, Acts 3:19).

In the same way that repurposing can give new life to old things, spending time with Christ through Bible meditation and prayer can breathe new life into worn and weary souls. Because of His tenderness toward us and His desire to fellowship with us, Christ doesn't give up on us when we struggle. The Scripture says we may stumble, but we will not fall if we are holding onto Him. He seeks us out in order to restore and renew our faltering faith.

"Maybe your life has changed dramatically and you can't find a reason or purpose for being on earth. When God makes a vessel for His use, He may redesign, remold, rebuild, recast, recycle, or repurpose it, but you can be sure it's never discarded or destroyed. As long as the vessel is willing to remain a vessel, there is always a purpose for its existence" (http://favored1-dailyfavor.blogspot.com/2014/05/repurposed-christians.html).

God's grace can be rekindled every day! "Because of the Lord's faithful love, we do not perish, for His mercies never end. They are new every morning; great is Your faithfulness!" (Lam. 3:22–23, HCSB).

THE MOST IMPORTANT THING ABOUT FAITH

When the Bible speaks of faith, it tells us that there is something even greater that we need in our life. "If I have the gift of prophecy, and know all mysteries and all knowledge, and if I have all faith as to move mountains, but do not have love, I am nothing" (1 Cor. 13:2, NASB). In verse 13, it goes on to say that there is hope, faith, and love, and the greatest of these is love.

Repurposed faith without love is nothing. But repurposed faith centered in God's love is everything. "Sow righteousness for your-selves. Reap the fruit of unfailing love, and break up your unplowed ground, for it is time to seek the Lord, until He comes and showers his righteousness on you" (Hosea 10:12, NIV). Faith expresses itself through love (Galatians 5:6).

As I finish this book designed to help you grow closer to God in your personal moments with Him, I do so by offering a prayer for you and myself as well.

A PRAYER

Dear Heavenly Father,

Thank You for inviting us into a personal relationship with You. Show Yourself to us in such a powerful way that we will be drawn into Your holy presence many times throughout our days and weeks. May our practice of hav-ing a daily quiet time be more than something we check off a to-do list but rather a dynamic foundation for our entire life. May we be obedient to You and resist the devil so that he will flee. Show us how to be dressed and ready with Your armor on, so that we may stand firm when our earthly knees get weak. When we stumble and all hope seems gone, forgive us and lift us up with renewed hope. May we sit in Your light, offering You praise. As we read Your Word, may we pray it back to You and in so doing, draw close to Your heart. Above all Father, thank You for Your love for us, that You see us and that we matter to You. May we have that same kind of love for others so our faith will be real and authentic. Lead us according to Your purpose for our lives. Move us past lukewarm to warm and then on to red-hot in our love for You. May You be our passion, not things or money or status. May You satisfy our dry souls, as we look to You. Reveal mysteries hidden in Your Word, and may our meditation lead us to deeper times of prayer. Help us to be doers of the Word and not just hearers. Thank You that when we are weak, You are strong. As we draw close to You, may You draw close to us and show us Your ways. We know that days will look different, life may take its toll, and losses will be hard, but help us to follow close in Your footsteps and show us the meaning of having an abundant life in You. In Jesus' name, Amen.

Wait! What's that Lord? You are inviting us all to dinner? A banquet? A feast? Help us to RSVP with a resounding "yes!"

AN INVITATION TO GOD'S BANQUET TABLE

We have all been invited to dine at Christ's table. In Psalm 23, He prepared a table for David in the presence of his enemies. His enemies could only observe as David's head was anointed with oil, which was a traditional gift given to esteemed guests. His cup was more than full; it was overflowing. In the same way, God wants us to feast at His table, no matter our situation. He is a gracious host who shepherds His people with care, meeting us at our point of need. Not only did the Good Shepherd provide for David's physical needs, He led him to a place of rest and quiet, and then He restored his soul . . . repurposed his faith . . . not for a day or a week, but an act of loving-kindness that followed David all the days of his life.

"While a shepherd provides his sheep with food, rest, and restoration, God provides His sheep with His Word, which is the principle means of giving spiritual nourishment, rest, and restoration. Goodness and loving-kindness are probably the two most comforting attributes of God's character for the Christian. They are especially consoling in times of distress. As a guest at God's table, his enemies no longer stalk David; instead, God's goodness pursues him. God not only walks before us, leading us to places of rest and refreshment, but His goodness follows us from behind as well" (www.Bible.org).

As I was thinking about banquet tables, my mind immediately went to an unlikely one! It was my grade school lunchroom table, where I sat glowing, looking up at my daddy date, just so happy that he came all dressed up to the father-daughter banquet. Knowing my dad wanted to spend this time with me, I felt special.

A few weeks ago, I read a news article where a bride was stood up at the altar. Bouncing back from her heartache over her fiancé's no-show, she and the wedding party headed out to the streets in search of homeless folks to invite to the high-end wedding reception where they all had quite the feast. In Luke 14:16, a man prepared a great feast and sent out many invitations. When he sent his servant to tell the people that the banquet dinner was ready, one by one they began giving excuses as to why they couldn't come. The unhappy master sent his servant into the streets and alleys of the town and invited those from the streets to come in and enjoy the feast, giving them all a place of honor at his table.

As we think about God knocking on the door of our heart, waiting to invite us to dine with Him, let us open that door with eager expectation. "Look! I stand at the door and knock. If you hear my voice and open the door, I will come in, and we will share a meal together as friends" (Rev. 3:20, NLT). My prayer is that as we draw close and listen during that dinner conversation, we will hear in our hearts and spirits the individual, God-designed purpose He has for each one of us. May we allow the Spirit of the Living God to breathe new life into our quiet time, and may we never be the same.

For more information about

Rosie Williams

and
Repurposed Faith
please visit:

rosiejwilliams.com
rosemarywilliams6@icloud.com
@rosiejwilliams
www.facebook.com/roseyjwilliams

For more information about
AMBASSADOR INTERNATIONAL
please visit:

www.ambassador-international.com
@AmbassadorIntl
www.facebook.com/AmbassadorIntl

More from Ambassador International

It's time to take a deep breath and do some inventory. Let's dig in and see what God's Word has to say about this tug-of-war between our flesh and our mission. Let's figure out ways to quit chasing emptiness and take bold steps of obedience. Let's discover how we can glorify God and steer people to Jesus in our cubicles, at our dinner tables, in our mom-groups, and with people we encounter every day.

What would happen if we said Enough of Me . . . more Jesus.

As we walk through dark times in our lives, we all need a way of finding truth in the tempest. Whether we are asking "Why the Tempest?" or struggling when life doesn't make sense, God's Word is sufficient to answer all of our questions.

This devotional journal is not meant to be read as a daily plan, and instead offers meditations on Scripture to help for your unique circumstance.

Explore this collection of real-life experiences and glimpses into a woman's personal relationship with God. Discover for yourself what the Women of the Secret Place have learned. As you relax with the fifty-two devotionals in *Women of the Secret Place*, you will laugh, cry, and be encouraged. You will gain new appreciation for God's unique plan for you as a woman of faith. You will be inspired to trust Him through life's most difficult circumstances!

Made in the USA
Monee, IL
07 May 2024